Humanification

Humanification

CHRISTIAN KROMME

THE CHOIR PRESS

First published in the United Kingdom in 2017 by
The Choir Press

ISBN 978-1-910864-97-5

Contents

Acknowledgements

I would like to thank my wife Petra for standing beside me throughout my career and while writing this book. She has been my inspiration and motivation for continuing to improve my knowledge and move my career forward. When I was writing, she did all the rest! I also thank my three wonderful children, Lieke, Pepijn, and our new addition Ruben, for inspiring me and always making me smile, and for their understanding on all those times when I was writing this book instead of spending time with them. I hope that one day they can read this book and understand why I spent so much time in front of my computer. I'd like to thank my parents for allowing me to follow my ambitions throughout my childhood. I also want to thank Ad Nederlof for taking the time and effort to write the foreword of this book and for inspiring me to write this book in the first place! I also want to thank the community around me and all the people in the audiences I was honoured to speak to. You all played your part in giving me valuable reflection and feedback that has undoubtedly improved the content of this book.

Last, but definitely not least, I'd like to thank Sophie Bennett.[1] Sophie has provided excellent editorial support, inspiration, advice, and a lot of patience and perseverance during the writing of this book. Without her efforts this book simply wouldn't have had the form and structure to make the ideas complete, and her turn of phrase and storytelling skills breathed life into much of the science. Sophie, I could not have done it without you. Thanks for everything, and let's get to work on the second edition soon!

Also, many thanks to Miles and his team at Choir Press for getting the final manuscript to print.

---

[1] www.sophiebennett.com

Foreword

Several years ago, somewhere around October 2014, my companions at the VANAD Group, Arthur Nederlof and Arnoud Munneke, asked if I could adjust my schedule in order to meet Christian Kromme.

After I questioned who Kromme was, my companions gave me a short explanation: 'Christian is the founder of a relatively small but extremely innovative company. The company, Artificial Industry, specialises in making human-centred design and making human-centric online platforms and mobile apps. VANAD lacks this kind of knowledge, therefore we were very eager to partner with them.'

When Christian entered my office, I was expecting to see a man who wanted to conquer the world of business and with the simple interest of earning money quickly.

During our meeting, we didn't talk about money or about 'exit' strategies, but about increasing technology and the impact this would have on a community and the individual in the community. It was all about changes; they are on our doorstep right now, they are happening today in our homes, our companies and our jobs. They are changing the way we shop, eat, communicate, how we empower our lives, and how we connect to the outside world.

The hour I had reserved to meet Christian quickly turned into several hours. I had the growing feeling that the entrepreneur I thought was sitting in front of me was actually someone who could improve the world greatly. A modern philosopher who really understands how and what will change in the future and when these changes will happen. This wasn't based on the superficial wisdoms that many would harass you with; it was based on well thought through concepts, some of which he already had experience with.

Towards the end of the conversation, Christian confirmed my conclusion. He said: 'Don't see me as the man who has only one objective of making Artificial Industry a large and successful company. If everything goes to plan, I will stop and do what has always been my passion, to give lectures and inform people about the things we have spoken about.'

The collaboration between the VANAD Group and Artificial Industry eventually resulted in the VANAD Group taking over the company.

While Christian was in charge, new projects were starting to form. For example, there was the development of a new and unique 3D flower arranging cloud application that we named Bloomy Pro.

Another example was a disruptive digital platform for the green industry, and there are many more projects in development. Due to Artificial Industry's rapid growth, they soon had to move to a larger office.

In March 2016, when Arnoud Munneke and I visited Artificial Industry, I asked Christian a few important questions. For example: 'When are you going to make your dream a reality?' and 'When are you going to share your vision with others through training programmes and lectures?'

'Perhaps at the end of this year,' he answered. 'There is still a lot of work to be done and that has to be done first.' I tried to explain that there is never a right time to take such steps in life and I suggested that he should make his ideas a reality immediately.

Somewhat astonished, he hesitatingly agreed and we called in his excellent second-in-command Jochem and told him that he more or less was in charge from that moment onwards. Naturally the transfer happened very smoothly although Christian is not the type to drop all of his responsibilities without taking great care.

So, Christian was, from that very moment forward, free to go where he wanted to go and to do what he thought was best. I also advised him to write a book through which he could expound his vision clearly. I, myself, have written a few books in the past, my most successful book being *Customer Obsession*. I wrote this book because, at the time in my role as CEO of Genesys, I was often asked to give presentations about how to reform a traditional organization into a 'customer-centric organization'. I thought, which was somewhat naïve of me, that the publication of this book containing my vision would mean there would be fewer requests for my lectures and presentations, but this proved to be otherwise; writing this book only increased the requests. The business community then started to introduce me as some kind of guru – something I knew I certainly was not and that Christian, in my opinion, would become.

Christian has, since the decision was made to pass on his business responsibilities, continued to develop the quality of his lectures and presentations whilst writing his book. Above all, he also remained very active in the ongoing research regarding the impact that technology has on the human being and our society and I can tell you that that impact is enormous.

Many jobs will be replaced by the rapid development of technology and at the same time prosperity and the amount of free time people have will increase.

It all seems contradictory but that is far from the truth. The word 'work' will have a different meaning and will not only be associated with earning a living.

Society will change and if these changes are managed properly by politicians and executives, then these changes will lead to a huge improvement in the quality of life on this planet.

Christian has a clear vision about these changes that he describes inside this book. The concept of Humanification comes alive in a captivating style as he explains how his vision can be applied in a specific context, a company, or even to an individual. That is how Christian inspired me, and he even contributed to changes in my lifestyle and as a result my health as a diabetic patient has improved dramatically.

For the past two and a half years Christian has inspired many employees within the VANAD Group with respect to software development. We have changed the way we do things.

His unique view of technology and its relationship with society and human beings characterises Christian and that makes reading his book a true experience and essential reading for all of us.

His vision will stay with you consciously or unconsciously; it will change your everyday life.

And that is exactly what Christian was aiming for. He has already thoroughly influenced me in a very positive way and for that I will always be grateful.

I hope that his book has the same effect on all of those who are fortunate enough to read it.

Ad Nederlof
Chairman of the VANAD Group and former CEO of Genesys

Part I
The Principles of Humanification

Chapter 1

Disrupt or Die

They told me my daughter was dying.

That day, I had no idea that such dreadful news would lead to a discovery that would revolutionise our understanding of innovation – what powers innovation, how it happens, how we can predict it and even make it happen.

The speed of innovation in technology is increasing, and it's going to totally transform our world. This book is about how we can harness its power to make our lives better, help businesses thrive and predict the next wave of change.

In this book, I'll explain how to recognise and tune into the force that drives exponential trends. Businesses that align with this force behave in a certain way and evolve at exponential speeds, and it's a force that **you** can tap into.

From business to government, from medicine to computer networks, from personal intelligence to artificial intelligence; everything we think we know today is going to be transformed within our lifetime.

Join me on a journey that exposes some startling parallels between nature and technology.

Disruptive innovation has always been part of human development. We already know that it's the very essence of evolution in the natural world. What this book does is to reveal that nature and technology are much closer in evolutionary terms than you might think. Startlingly close, in fact.

A healthy human body is a social and coherent community of over 10 trillion cells that work together seamlessly. So what does this have to do with technology? Perhaps more than you think . . .

We can learn a great deal from the cells in our body; how they communicate with each other, how they organise and solve complex problems by working together in social, coherent, and efficient communities. There's nothing random about the solutions created by organic life, and when you look closely these systems help to explain the exponential trends we see everywhere around us in our man-made world. Nature also teaches us how we can make technology more human – a concept I've termed Humanification.

Humanification shines a light into your future, the future of business, and of our collective potential, and it's a future that's less unpredictable than you might think.

Nature gives us predictive powers, when we know where to look for the clues. The challenges currently faced by families, entrepreneurs, employees, business leaders, our communities and even policymakers and governments can be explained and solved when you understand the principles of Humanification.

The natural patterns of life and the technological developments that affect us all really can be explained. We have the ability to transform our personal well-being, our businesses, our communities, our societies and even our environment with this new understanding.

Together we'll explore the previously hidden patterns that shape our world so we can harness them and be less fearful of the future.

There are truly remarkable parallels between our own biology and our man-made technology – parallels that have already transformed all of our lives, and things are only just getting started.

The driving forces behind the miracle of organic life are coded patterns that could have predicted the internet, Facebook, Uber and many more 'surprises' that have taken the world by storm.

This book will help you to makes sense of our rapidly changing world and harness a new understanding to help you, your family, company, and community to adapt and thrive.

Disruptive innovation is no longer the exception, it's the new normal; and change is hotting up.

Make no mistake, big changes are on the horizon. The waves of change are swelling. You can't see most of them, but they are there . . . and some of them are tsunamis.

These monster waves will almost certainly wipe out some things that you hold dear, but they have equal power to help us to replace what's lost with something much better.

I believe that Nature shows us that governments are going to become less powerful, collective intent and intelligence will become unstoppable, and the businesses and companies of the future will look very different indeed. The world of work is going to change beyond recognition and being ready will help you and the people you care about thrive, as long as you are open and ready for what's coming next.

The changes are already on your doorstep; they are happening today in your home, your company, and your job. They are changing the way you shop, eat, communicate, how you power your life, and how you connect to the outside world.

This is your opportunity to gain insight into where the next big wave is going to come from, and where it's going to take you.

Humanification is more than just an idea; it's a new wave of understanding that helps to make sense of what's driving technology, what's in store for a new more collaborative society, and how we do business in the future.

You will find out why the essence of life really is information. You will gain a new perspective on technology, how we all interact with it, and where it's going next.

We are going to start by looking at and understanding the parallels between our own biology and twenty-first century technology. We'll explore the 7 biological waves of evolution and reveal the surprising patterns that almost perfectly map to the technology that sits in your pocket and powers your home.

You will find out just how much technology is going to change everything and just how fast those changes are going to happen. You'll start to see how artificial intelligence (AI) is already guiding many aspects of our lives and where it's going to take us next.

The next wave is already driving some of the transformational businesses that have changed the way we all live and work. Just think back to the days before Google, Amazon or satnav. Although it's hard to remember, it wasn't very long ago. Many of these changes in our everyday lives have happened in a matter of months or a few short years, instead of over decades or centuries.

We will be looking at examples of how some businesses such as Google, Uber and many others could have been predicted if we had had our Human-ification glasses on. But we didn't, and they seemed to surprise almost everybody. We are entering into the new era that's coming at breathtaking speed and the more human our technology becomes, the faster those changes to our businesses and everyday lives are going to happen.

So let's start at the beginning with how it all started; how one little girl's close call with death was to be the tipping point for a new predictive power for our future.

Chapter 2

Patterns, Parallels, and Time Machines

They had to perform heart surgery. On a three-month-old baby. That's an absolutely terrifying prospect for any parent. But it was after the surgery that things got really scary. Five times the white-coated medical team tried to take our daughter off the heart-lung machine, but her heart-lung function just wouldn't start up again.

The doctors pumped her full of medication and, finally, at the sixth attempt, her heart and lungs started to function again. Her life had been saved, but the relief wasn't going to last.

Later that evening, we got the news.

It was a rare genetic disorder, they said.

It was incurable, they said.

We were stunned. We almost lost her coming out of surgery, then this.

Then came the real blow: 'We have to follow protocol. You need to know that we won't resuscitate your daughter when she deteriorates. We are very sorry to tell you this, but we won't be giving Lieke a bed in the intensive care unit after she has had her surgical recovery time. She isn't entitled to one.'

You might be wondering why I'm sharing this with you. It's because it was only through Lieke's illness, and the search for something that would extend her life and give her quality of life worth having, that led to many of the discoveries you are going to uncover in this book.

The hospital protocol didn't allow intensive care beds to be occupied by children with a prognosis of death. If life expectancy is lower than three per cent, it's just not allowed under the rules, and our daughter didn't have the required three per cent. So after a staggeringly slow recovery and six weeks in the intensive care unit, Lieke had to be transferred to a normal ward.

She did get lots of attention, but for all the wrong reasons. She was such a unique specimen for the doctors to study, so she had plenty of curious medical staff coming in to see this unusual little girl. Yet, bizarrely, every time there was a positive step or an improvement in her condition, the doctors seemed to find another reason why she wouldn't make it to her first birthday. Beliefs are a powerful predictor of behaviour, and their belief was that there was nothing that could make a difference.

The entire team, a dozen specialist doctors and even a second opinion from another academic hospital, all told the same story: she was going to die, and there was nothing they could do to help.

No innovation, just the acceptance of a sad reality. But I believe that is where much innovation happens. When there are no options and things just can't be accepted as they are – change becomes possible.

Our little baby girl was just three months old and she had just been given a life sentence. Top medical specialists were telling us that the genetic defect was so unusual that there were no success stories for us to study. All the known patients had died before their first birthday. I don't blame the doctors; they were just falling back on protocols and the medical system that they knew. How many businesses do that? It's not working, it can't be fixed, the competition is overtaking them, so they just give up or pretend that the problem will just go away ...

The doctors just didn't have the time or the resources to look at the bigger picture and to see things from a new perspective.

Thankfully, I did. That sort of news both sharpens the mind and dents your faith in the system, but it also opens the mind to looking into new approaches and looking outwards to the margins of medicine and science – even if the potential solutions aren't conventionally accepted. That principle applies to all innovation. It's much more likely to happen on the margins than in the mainstream.

Our instincts told us that the answers weren't going to be found in hospital and that the medical system was actually making our daughter more and more sick.

So we took her home. Home became an intensive care unit. We had a team of fifteen different nurses coming in and out to help, a house filled up with medical equipment and medicines. We could have opened a pharmacy. We were doing everything possible to buy some time while we tried to find a different approach.

I studied day and night. Between books and machines, the wires and tubes connected up to her struggling body, and mountains of information on the internet, I managed to start to make headway and start connecting some rather unusual dots and saw a new picture emerging.

The dots weren't easy to see at first because most innovations were coming from within the healthcare industry itself – the very bubble of thinking that had predicted that she would die. It quickly became obvious that established medical thinking was being restricted by what they already knew.

I had to go outside the system to find out about a groundbreaking new treatment technology. More about that later.

You see, looking for both patterns and exceptions had been my job for the previous thirteen years. I could never have imagined that my studies and my research into innovation and AI would ever help me in the matter of the life or death of my own daughter, but, surprisingly, it helped a great deal.

I was lucky to have studied at Hogeschool Utrecht University of Applied Sciences on a degree course that was revolutionary at the time. My studies were a combination of three subjects: creativity, technology, and entrepreneurship.

That unique study path was instrumental to me founding my company in 2002. That business helped companies and entrepreneurs to dramatically speed up their rate of innovation. It was time to bring that experience to my family and attempt to use it to save a life.

My business was all about making complex things simple and understandable again to real people, and to make technology more 'human', or, as some people term it, user-friendly. My business served many big customers like Philips, Bjorn Borg, Adidas, EMI, Toyota, Oracle, Shell, and Endemol.

Being innovative was in the DNA of that business. Yet it wasn't until my own family life suffered a major disruption that turned our world upside down that I finally understood how easy it is to for people to retreat to the comfort zone and look to the establishment for help.

Finally, I understood the resistance I had witnessed over the years from our clients, but I also realised the true value of what we did.

When a child is dying in front of your eyes, disrupting and challenging established ideas and innovating takes on a whole new dimension.

So it was time to apply the very approach I had championed as a professional disrupter and innovator and to use it to see if my daughter's life could be saved.

It was beyond doubt that it was impossible to get new answers by looking in old places. It was the discoveries I made during that frantic search that joined biology and technology in ways I couldn't have imagined before Lieke's illness. Some of the revelations started to make more sense of things my company had already been using in businesses and I was able to see why they worked at a deeper level than ever before, and some were totally new. These discoveries would not only be instrumental in saving my daughter's life, but would also have the power to help us to see where technology is going taking us in the future, and even predict the pace of change.

I uncovered strange parallels between the way our cells function and the way technology works. I discovered that information really is the key to life (and, more to the point, why that matters so much) and that the evolution of artificial intelligence and the inherent intelligence that allows life to thrive are connected. In fact, they are more than connected; in many ways, they mirror each other.

So it's time to start an incredible journey through time. You are going to understand how these two worlds collide and that we can use this knowledge to visualise the future of humankind and apply the patterns that I discovered to the advancement of technology. And that, dear reader, will have massive implications for just about every aspect of our own lives and the lives of our children and grandchildren.

Imagine you are sitting in a one-cell time machine and put your seat belt on. You are about to understand why the pace of change is going to increase at an almost unimaginable speed, how it's going to affect the way that you live and work in the next two, five, ten years and beyond.

Chapter 3
The Biology of Technology

As humans, we so often think that what we are doing is 'unnatural', and yet when the patterns of our technology are revealed, that very idea is turned on its head. In fact, technology couldn't have adapted much **more** naturally. This book (and my work when I'm working directly with organisations) revolves around a single core idea of making things as natural as they really want to be. We humans are instinctive creatures; it's locked in our biology, and man-made technological innovation follows the patterns of nature because we are natural. When we see evidence of it and when we start to believe it, we can make faster progress and have an increased likelihood that the ideas we are doing are best to develop get traction in the marketplace.

The way nature works is really quite simple and elegant. All we need to do is understand the driving forces that allow innovation to take place, and tap into them.

This simple observation is that the development and evolution of technology has mirrored nature in almost every way as far back as we can look in history. When you recognise those patterns – and see how nature has created its own problems, solved them and moved on through the cycle of development – you realise that predicting what is coming next isn't as difficult or complex as you might think. I call it 'the biology of technology'.

> **Biology** provides us with a blueprint of how we can use **technology** to build a social, coherent and sustainable **humanity.** The more human and natural technology feels to the user, the faster this building process can take place. This is the concept of **Humanification.**

This isn't just an idea; it's been happening all around us for generations, and it can help us shape – and even predict – what our future is going to look like. To fully grasp where the ideas and understanding of these patterns can take us, we first need to look backwards in time to see where the patterns come from, and why they exist. Without that understanding you aren't fully equipped to anticipate what's coming next. When you are able to connect the dots yourself, you have the power to use the patterns to project forward and make predictions and plan for the future that's coming. And, as you are going to see, the future is coming faster than we have ever experienced in history. That's not a statement I make to make the prose sound good – it's a fact, and I'm going to prove it to you by sharing my research with you.

There is a Pattern to Everything

There are patterns that already exist in almost every element of life on earth (and many of the patterns we see elsewhere in the universe too), and I came to realise that those same patterns apply to technology as well as nature, even though it's not obvious at first investigation. Like nature, the sheer number of variables available can at first seem mind-boggling, but when you stand back far enough and see the patterns, the sheer simplicity and elegance becomes obvious.

The journey we are going to take together is all based around this simple concept. Together we will see the beauty, oddity, logic, and the inevitability of what's coming next.

There are so many strange comparisons and layers to understand before you can really harness the true predictive power of these insights. It's like a jigsaw; at first you can only see the individual pieces and it can take a little while to see the bigger picture. As the parts start to come together, the whole picture emerges out of the complexity, and your own understanding of the pieces emerges at the same time. It all starts to make sense.

So let's start with the building blocks of life, then dig further down into the strange and truly bizarre nature of patterns and complexity. After that, we can zoom back out to the simplicity and clarity in a way that makes sense. Everything will make so much more sense when you understand the relationships between all the facts and concepts. You will have what you need to join the dots and understand the stages of innovation and see what part of the pattern and cycle we are currently in as a society. You will be able to see where you are in the cycle – personally, in business is right now, and in terms of governments and how we are ruled. You will be able to spot threats or opportunities that are out there waiting. The principles are going to reveal much about your personal future and the future of humanity itself. We live in exciting times, and you are about to find out just how exciting things are going to get – and how quickly it's going to happen.

'Nothing is more powerful than an idea whose time has come.'
– Victor Hugo

Chapter 4

Physical Assets Zero – Cash Value Billions

Before you get into the really strange world that is the biology of technology, let's just take a quick look at where we are right now in terms of the speed of change we have experienced in recent years. Just a decade ago, the idea of how these companies would even exist, let alone make a profit, would have been unthinkable. Yet today:

- The world's largest taxi company owns no taxis (Uber)
- The largest accommodation provider owns no real estate (Airbnb)
- The largest phone company owns no telecoms infrastructure (Skype/WeChat)
- The world's most valuable retailer has no inventory (Alibaba)
- The most popular media owner creates no content (Facebook)
- One of the fastest growing banks has no actual money (SocietyOne)
- The largest software vendors don't write the majority of the available apps (Apple/Google)

So what's going on?

Change doesn't happen incrementally; it only appears to. At first you don't notice because the changes are so small that they often don't get spotted.

After all, as humans, we only process a small number of things at once on a conscious level. It's inevitable that we miss most of the signs. I'm going to share with you what to watch for. If you can see the early signs you have an opportunity to prepare and adapt, or, even better, be ahead of the curve that the majority are about to miss out on.

Disruptive companies like Spotify, Airbnb, Skype, and Netflix have had the skills to see where the next technology wave was swelling, and they were exactly where they needed to be at the right time and they leveraged the power of the wave. That gave them the disruptive opportunity to gain speed in comparison to traditional companies. If you know where the next wave will swell and what that wave will be, then you will have a disruptive advantage against your competitors. So how do you predict the wave?

Well, that's what this book is all about: understanding the pre-conditions that allow the wave to form and having an insight into the conditions that allow the wave to gain size and power.

If you wait and respond to the changing technological and business landscape – in other words, if you try to adapt to today's world as it happens – it won't be very long before you're too late.

Remember Alta Vista, anyone?

Being able to anticipate the future instead of reacting to what's happening now is going to be key to survival. Your company, your business and your job are on the line because change is happening so fast that everything is on the line (and it's speeding up every day, as you are about to find out).

People and businesses that are ready to pick up the pace of change faster than the rest won't just survive; they'll thrive. Those who don't will sadly be left in the backdraught, and will wonder what on earth has happened.

So let's look at the forces that drive change. We will start with something that's going to surprise you: nature and the fundamentals of evolution. Nature's forces are so close to the forces that are driving technological innovation and change that it's almost *beyond* spooky . . .

So to understand where technology is going, we need to start with a basic understanding of our biology – because the two are intrinsically linked by the forces of nature.

What you are about to discover will change the way you think about our future, and the speed of the next wave of changes as well. Because it's happening now – and there is so much happening out there that you probably aren't aware of yet. Science fiction is becoming science fact. Get ready for a whistle-stop tour of the past, an assessment of where we are right now, and a glimpse into the future. Get ready for Humanification.

Chapter 5
Disruption Secrets

So what about what's going on today? Is there a common pattern that disruptive companies have in common?

> *'You can't connect the dots looking forward; you can only connect them looking backwards. So you have to trust that the dots will somehow connect in your future.'*
>
> – Steve Jobs

Well, yes. There are a lot of things that they have in common; for example, the most disruptive (and often faster growing) companies build platforms that solve very complex problems and use smart technology. But that's not the biggest common factor. In fact, what they have in common is so simple to understand yet really difficult to do – and it's where I believe that businesses need to be doubling our efforts. The biggest thing the most successful companies do is to make technology more human-like.

They humanify technology so that a lot of people are going to use it. Uptake happens at lightning speed, because when you make technology more natural to use, when it feels more natural, you adapt more easily when you use the product. Consumers are getting used to great design – and if it doesn't feel natural, a product doesn't get traction; and if it does get traction (despite poor design or an unnatural interface), it doesn't last long. The new kid on the block quickly gets disrupted by something that's better designed. The pioneer gets left in the dust while the improver gets most of the market share.

It's the Humanification of the design that gives these companies the disruptive edge and incredible speed of development and growth. More about what that actually means as we go through the book. When a product or technology is humanified well, lots of people start to use it, and the speed of uptake gives the company a massive advantage against companies who haven't got human-friendly technology.

Take the iPad as an example. Apple's iPad is a great example of making technology more human-like. A two-year-old child can play with it without being able to read a user manual or navigate to a help file. Almost everyone can grasp an iPad with an app in minutes. It doesn't matter if the user is mentally or physically disabled – almost everyone can work it out using their instincts. Yet that doesn't make it so basic that it's not of high commercial value. Professionals can work with it and run a business from almost anywhere. Smartphones are going the same way.

These devices make technology so accessible and feel so natural that they are easily adapted by the target audience. That gave Apple the advantage, and the primary advantage that counts these days is the speed of innovation – not just the quality of it.

The first to market with a humanified product that disrupts the market gains a huge advantage; the company that comes second has an uphill struggle to survive.

Even a message can be humanified. You talk about technical data and it isn't very appealing or human. You talk about the emotional benefits and it suddenly connects to real people. Technology, products, videos, and ideas all go viral for the same reason – they are humanified. Sometimes by design, sometimes by accident.

In my field of work, I have inevitably talked to a lot of people about 'disruptive innovation', and what I found out is that a lot of people say, 'okay, disruption. Yeah, I know something about Uber and it has disrupted the taxi industry,' but they think it's far away and it's not coming to their business/job/life that soon. But that's a misunderstanding and a gross miscalculation; one that I hope that you won't be making. That's because disruption is like a chain reaction. It starts in a small way, then it follows a predictable pattern. Most people just don't see the small start and then they miss the pattern.

Uber's platform started a host of new taxis and sharing economy and it would be an understatement to say that it's worked out pretty well for Uber's ability to raise capital and connect drivers to passengers. In fact, it worked so well that 'to Uber' has even become a verb in the dictionary. Uber are now copying their concept and using it to disrupt the logistics industry.[2] (To

---

[2] https://www.wired.com/2016/10/ubers-self-driving-truck-makes-first-delivery-50000-beers/

speed up progress they bought an autonomous truck company and the first freight delivery was 50,000 cans of Budweiser beer.)

Uber are now able to deliver a package in thirty minutes to your front door. That idea has worked well too, so now they are copying that same formula yet again, this time to the fresh goods industry, so your fresh meal will be delivered within thirty minutes to your front door. The Uber division is called Ubereats and already has restaurant and delivery partners across continents; you can get your favourite food, from Brussels to Bogota, delivered to your door.

So what's next?

Is your job or business as safe as you thought it was five minutes ago? If you thought that these disruptive little upstarts aren't going to come to your town or city, think again. They are probably there already – even if you haven't spotted them yet.

Once there is some kind of problem that's solved and a disruptive idea has been successfully tested on the market, then it's copied or adapted very quickly into other industries and other markets. A level of cross-fertilization of ideas has always happened for as long as we have been using technology, but what's different today is the speed at which it's happening because of the internet and the growing processing speed and power of our computing. You will be looking at this in much more detail as you progress through the book. But for now, just be assured that the cycle is running at a different pace this time, and we are going somewhere new with it.

For example, look at the story behind iTunes. iTunes was disrupted by Spotify. Yet it was iTunes itself that disrupted the music market.

Apple's iTunes platform turned the traditional music market on its head. The old way, with its physical music carriers and old-style thinking, didn't know what had hit them when Apple made music a **virtual product**.

For the first time, with iTunes you could download your music. But that wasn't the end of it. One upstart disrupted another. Spotify came along and disrupted Apple. They changed the business model so instead of giving you one song at a time and having you pay for it, Spotify took the same digital product and gave customers an unlimited amount of music for a fixed fee each month. It rocked the entire industry (excuse the pun), including the tech company that changed the business model.

That same disruptive model for digitised media was rapidly copied to other industries, and soon the video and movie industry had to flex their models and adapt to changing customer expectations.

With Netflix, you can watch unlimited movies for $10 a month. You can read unlimited news, magazine, or book titles for a fixed price per month. Amazon Prime has moved into the space, of course, and much of the expensive testing had already been done before Mr Bezos rolled that one out. The early pioneers must have saved him a fortune in market testing.

A lot of business models are copied or simply lightly adapted and transferred to other industries. If you wait until your neighbour is metaphorically on fire, then you're certainly too late and are likely to be burned to a crisp.

Eventually, I believe every industry will be disrupted. I say that because, in some way, every market, every industry, is connected to others, because we humans are highly connected to each other.

If something happens in one market area, it will certainly be copied. The first one takes a while, but the second copy is much faster, so every industry in the future and every business will be digital. You will start to see that when a business becomes digital it is going to be disrupted one way or another; probably sooner rather than later.

There are going to be big knock-on effects across whole industries. For example, when humans drive cars we have a habit of damaging our vehicle roughly every 100,000 km. Yet when we have robot cars, we are already seeing accident rates plummet to damage every 10,000,000 km driven. That statistic will reduce even further as the technology improves, and the first thing we could see is a hybrid of autonomous technology. That's where you will still be driving your car, but in the event of a looming accident, the car will intervene and save you just in time.

All these changes are going to have a massive effect. Just think about it. What's it going to do to the bodyshop industry? There's going to be a lot less work: replacement parts suppliers will be hit, car paint manufacturers will have less paint to make. Spray shops will have less to do and the businesses that supply those companies will also feel the effects. The ripple effects from these changes are going to be massive. Are you in an industry that's a prime target for disruption? It's well worth thinking forward to get a feeling for the threats to your business or your job because change really is just around the next corner. There will be opportunities too, though, and these are limited only by your imagination and flexibility.

Chapter 6

Your Body is a Blueprint for Man-Made Technology

You really do work at the speed of light. It might sound bizarre, but it's exactly how your body works. Now, if you're thinking that this book is all about the future of where technology is taking us, and you're wondering why we are suddenly talking about the human body, stay with me because the parallels between biology and technology aren't just fascinating; they're the key to predicting what's coming in our future world.

This evolution isn't just going to affect our gadgets: it's going to affect everything from how we are governed to how we live and work. I believe that it's only possible to fully grasp the magnitude of the changes that are on the way by understanding the powerful forces that are at work right now.

Imagine for a moment you are a single cell. You want to tell your cell buddy next to you that something is going on outside. This is how you do it. You buzz over to him by using a series of electromagnetic signals. You do it by using a tiny light particle called a biophoton. Your external cell membrane, your cell's skin, can send and receive 100,000 light pulses **per second**. Your body really does work at the speed of light, and it won't be long before technology works just as fast. We are already closer than you think.

The biophysicist, Professor Fritz-Albert Popp, discovered this principle in the 1980s and 1990s, following on from the discovery of biophotons by Alexander Gurwitsch in 1923, but it's only more recently that its full force can be understood and applied to predictions of what's going to happen next in the field of technology. So how is this all connected? Well, I first came across it when Lieke was sick and I was looking for a potential cure.

I found out about a groundbreaking new treatment technology called biophoton therapy, where the cells of the body were treated with biophotons (light particles).

Now, you already know that you and your cell buddies communicate with tiny light particles. So now scale things up a bit from you as a single cell, to you as a whole human. Although at full size we don't appear to work quite that fast at a conscious level, in principle we do work in the same way as all our cells do, in terms of our behaviours.

For example, at least 85% of your communication is non-verbal. Other people take meaning from your facial expressions and your gestures in real time. The photons of light that illuminate your behaviour are reflected by your body into their eyes. Only a tiny part of your communication with other people is verbal. You both send and receive information with other people when you are with them in exactly the same way as your cells do, mostly through your 'cell membrane', your physical exterior. When all is going well, information travels freely.

Now, here's something interesting to understand. When single cells are in stress, the cell membrane closes and they go into rescue mode, the cell wall thickens and the cells reduce communication with other cells. That has the effect of allowing the cell to receive less information from their environment. That reduces their ability to adapt and react, and human beings behave in exactly the same way. When we are under threat we shut down. We are less open in our communication, and we also are less able to receive information. We shut down, just like our cells shut down.

Conversely, when a cell is relaxed, its cell membrane starts to thin and the cell absorbs information from its environment, and single cells start to multiply and to socialize. Humans do exactly the same.

Just like people, cells adjust to their environment. Did you know that if you place a healthy cell into a stressful and unhealthy environment, the cell will become ill, and when you put a sick cell in a healthy and stress-free environment the cell starts to recover?

Professor Bruce H. Lipton, a specialist in cell biology, discovered that cells rewrite their DNA all the time and adjust to their surroundings. Your DNA is not fixed, like traditional medical science has been telling us. If you want to find out more about this research, then check out the work being done in the field of epigenetics.

A healthy and stress-free human body is a coherent and social community of 10 trillion cells that work together seamlessly. If stress occurs beyond a certain point, then the cells inside our body reduce their communication with their neighbour and problems start to occur.

When you think about communities of people, they react in just the same way. For example, if you have two colleagues in a company department who don't communicate, trouble soon starts to appear. If the communication issue isn't solved quickly the problem can infect the whole department, the same way as an illness can eventually affect the whole body.

So back to Lieke. With the discovery of biophoton therapy we had a ray of hope.

(Don't you think it's interesting how we use that language, *a ray of hope*, to describe healing and other positive things? I believe we know more in our intuition and inner wisdom than our busy selves often have time to acknowledge. When we see someone who is in great health we often say how they are 'shining' or their eyes look 'bright'.)

So we decided to start with the controversial biophoton treatment, and after just two treatments we could see an improvement. After three treatments we saw a bigger shift. We were astonished about the positive effect it had on our daughter's health. It was like a miracle, and where my research was going to take me as a result was going to teach me a great deal about disruption, biology, technology, and the principles of Quantum Innovation.

Chapter 7

When Will You be able to Buy a Brain?

It's 2022. You are on a rare trip to a bricks-and-mortar store. You walk in, and you go straight to the counter with $1,000 in your hand (if real currency still exists in 2022 . . .) ready to spend on a new computer chip, to replace the one that just got eaten by the cat. How much processing power do you think your $1,000 will buy you in 2022?

If Ray Kurzweil, the director of the AI department at Google, is right, you will be able to buy the same processing power as a human brain with your $1,000. If you think that sounds a little crazy, it's because most of us are thinking in a linear way about the speed of technology progression; and I'm going to reveal why.

Ray Kurzweil didn't just pluck that prediction out of the air, and that's less far-fetched as a prediction than you might think. Kurzweil plotted all the improvements in information technology from 1900 in a graph, and looked at the rate of change. In 1900, there were no computers as we know them today, but there were mechanical computation machines, and they were able to process information in some way or another. He mapped processing power against equivalent levels of intelligence that we can relate to, and the rate of change is startling.

Between 1900 and the year 2000 we had barely managed to grow our processing power from a single unit up to the power of just one insect brain. But the growth curve was steady throughout the period, and when you take into account the odd interruption of wars and recessions, the growth curve followed a predicable shape and rate of change. The curve of the growth of processing power showed a remarkable pattern and rate of predictability.

We are going to be talking a lot about curves in this book. They are irrefutable patterns in both nature and technology. The curve Kruzweil plotted strongly suggests that by 2005 we would be comfortably processing the equivalent power to the brain of a mouse, a pretty complex animal when you compare it to a mosquito. And we were barely doing that at the turn of the century. That's not long ago. The curve keeps rising steeply, and by around 2022 the pattern suggests we will be able to have $1,000 of processing power equivalent of the human brain. Then, by the continuing doubling of power, by somewhere around 2040 a single unit would likely have the power of **all human brains on earth combined**. Where it goes after that in the next ten or twenty years is enough to bake anybody's noodle.

The acceleration process in not linear at all, but most of us are still thinking in a linear way despite the fact that technology is changing exponentially.

The difference between those two mindsets is what I call the Quantum Innovation[3] (QI) mindset.

That's a mindset that 'gets' what exponential growth actually means. A mindset that 'gets' the possibility of lots of parallel processes going on at the same time in different places, and understands that this is the mechanics that contribute to a series of rapid new developments.

To appreciate the power of exponential growth, and the potential for QI thinking, you need to start to appreciate the power of what exponential really means, because processing the concept isn't easy for the human brain. We aren't wired for exponential.

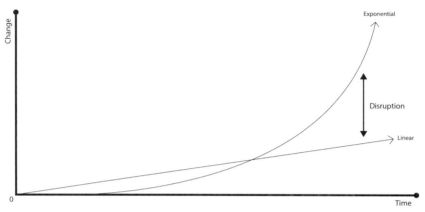

Figure 1: The power of an exponential mindset vs the limitations of linear thinking

---

[3] http://www.forbes.com/sites/offwhitepapers/2014/08/21/if-it-isnt-disruptive-
    innovation-then-what-is-it-try-quantum-innovation-on-for-size/#25b5598a3f52

Dr Albert Bartlett did a great deal of research on population growth, and he said that a lot of people don't understand how exponential functions work, which was restricting thinking on just how fast we were going to explode as a species. But he also wisely pointed out that nature is full of exponential functions, so if you want to get a handle on what the future has in store for us, it helps to start to understand it.

Just imagine for a moment that you are sitting in the Yankee Stadium in New York. It's a big stadium seating over 50,000 people. You look up at the clock and see that it's exactly twelve noon.

You have one drop of water on the palm of your hand, and that drop of water doubles every minute. After a couple of minutes, it becomes a bigger droplet. Now, in your mind, place the droplet in the middle of the stadium.

The drop starts doubling, and you are sitting on the upper ring of this huge stadium. How long do you think we have until the water is close enough for you to need to stop sitting and start swimming?

It's just fifty minutes.

By 12:50, the pool of water has doubled again and the stadium is completely filled to the brim.

But here's the scary thing about exponential growth – or put in its most basic terms, a continuous doubling.

At 12:45 the stadium was still 93% empty. So at 12:45 you would probably still be sitting quite happily thinking that nothing's really happening, ordering more cola and popcorn because it wouldn't look like the water was going to get you any time soon. Yet, in just five more minutes you wouldn't be eating your popcorn: you would be floating round the stadium with it swirling around your ears.

I believe that we are at 12:45 in technology terms right at this moment in time. We are at a time where a tsunami of technology is coming at us, and we are looking to the past, thinking that future shifts are going to happen at the same rate as they did in our lifetime – but it won't be that way.

The doubling of computing and networking power is compounding. What we are witnessing, without seeing it most of the time, is a huge flood of technological innovation coming at us. There's so much going on outside our daily awareness that we don't see the ripples. We mentally delete the small stuff – we haven't got time for it.

But it's a tsunami of small stuff, and it's about to hit.

So hold on to your popcorn because next we are going to dive deep into that water together. It's time to reveal the awesome compounding power of the S-curve and how it affects the future of everything we **think** we know (but don't) ...

Chapter 8

How a Drop of Water can Drown an Industry

In 1975 Steven Sesson, an engineer at Kodak, invented the first digital camera. He presented it to the board of Kodak, and they weren't as impressed as he'd hoped. They, in essence, sent him back to a lab in the basement. They didn't believe that digital would be the future. They did launch the camera, but soon dropped it due to the fear that it had the capacity to wipe out their traditional film business. You can almost imagine the conversation.

'Listen, Steve. We are a company and a brand that stands for quality. We are known for high-quality photographs, and 0.01 megapixels is not high quality. It's black and white, it takes twenty-six seconds to save the photo and another twenty-six seconds to read it back from the cassette. We don't understand this technology, so go back to your Research & Development department and think about something else.'

Kodak planned a ten-year-long transition to digital. The 1976 Kodak digital camera weighed in at 1.75 kg and cost the equivalent of approx. 10,000 euros. By 2014, a chip for a digital camera that weighed in at less than 0.001 kg (making it 1000 times lighter), with a memory capacity of over 10 megapixels (making it 1000 times more powerful), came in 1,000 times cheaper at just 10 euros. Multiply the improvements and the 2014 version is one billion times (that's 1000 x 1000 x 1000 times) better, and the chip is so tiny that it could sit on the head of a pin – and things have kept going since then. In technology terms, 2014 is already ancient history!

The co-authors of best selling books 'Abundance' and 'Bold', Peter H. Diamandis and Steven Kotler created a great framework called the 6Ds that has given life to some of the ideas in this book. Kotler's 6Ds are:

- Digitisation
- Deception
- Disruption
- Dematerialisation
- Demonetisation
- Democratisation

Big disruptive waves of change haven't been easy to predict. But there are clues. In the same way as an experienced surfer looking for a great wave to ride, when you know what to look for you can see a trend or disruption coming. There are signs out there. With the tools in this book you will have the ability to know what to look for in the next wave.

So let's surf those Ds in a bit more detail.

Phase One – Digitisation[4]

What they didn't understand at Kodak is that technology and information technology obeys Moore's law: it doubles every twelve to eighteen months. When information is digitised, it enters Phase One of the Quantum Innovation cycle. Just like a water droplet that fills a stadium in fifty minutes by constantly doubling, the speed and progression doesn't look relevant in the beginning.

Phase Two – The Big Deception

Back to the Kodak camera example. Research & Development (R&D) quickly moved capacity from 0.01 pixels to 0.02 pixels and only after ten or twelve doublings, the number of pixels became something that people started to really take notice of. That's a classic example of a moment when things move from being deceptive to disruptive.

The moment in time when people take notice of something that they previously dismissed is the moment that the true disruption happens. This is Phase Two; it's that point in time, the moment of disruption in action for

---

[4] Read more about Kotler's work at:
   http://bigthink.com/think-tank/steven-kotlers-six-ds-of-exponential-entrepreneurship

all to see. Yet, it's often still missed by many. The innovation has been happening all along, but like most tiny particles it's not noticed at the beginning. Cutler called it the deceptive phase because people who don't get it are deceived into thinking that nothing is really going on, when, in fact, there is a whole lot going on! When Kodak was going through challenges because of its late adoption of digital, they didn't see Instagram coming . . .

Phase Three – The Big Disruption

It's here when the innovation starts to take over. It's time for the big disruption. After ten or twelve doublings, you are entering what is often termed the knee of the curve (the stage at which an exponential trend becomes noticeable), and after this, progress is galloping forward very, very fast. We'll be talking more about curves in a later chapter because they are critical to understanding the circle of Quantum Innovation and your ability to be ahead of the curve.

For Kodak, this moment, after ten or twelve doublings in capacity, was the tipping point when many professional photographers switched from analogue cameras to digital cameras.

As with all 'sudden' shifts, it wasn't just the camera market that was affected, because those same photographers no longer needed to buy photographic film on rolls, they didn't need processing chemicals and they didn't need all the machinery required to develop the pictures either. An entire industry rushed headlong into bankruptcy because they didn't see the moment coming. They most definitely weren't riding the surf; they were sitting helplessly inside a sinking boat, and they went down with frightening speed. A company that had its origins going back to the Eastman Dry Plate Company, founded in 1881, found itself struggling for market share in the 1990s, cut almost 30,000 jobs during 2006/7 and filed for Chapter 11 bankruptcy in January 2012, having been the dominating force in the photographic film market for most of the twentieth century. That's how it often is with disruption. If you don't see the wave coming, or you try and surf it in the wrong boat, you'll go under.

Phase Four – Dematerialisation and Virtualisation

That might have been the end of the story for the Kodak business as we knew it, but it's not the end of the story.

In fact, it's just the beginning, because what happens next is Phase Four – that's when products become dematerialized; in other words, they become virtual. Not many years ago if you wanted to own a flashlight, a camera, a fax (now, there's a piece of ancient history for you …), a radio, a television or a satnav you had to buy a physical product. Now, all of those things sit in your pocket and exist as an app on your smartphone. They aren't material anymore. They have become dematerialised. They are virtual machines. The hardware that previously cost thousands of dollars is now virtual and almost for free.

Phase Five – Demonetisation

In Phase Five, what happens is that those apps will be developed by many other developers, they multiply, get cheaper and cheaper, and, eventually, they will be demonetised altogether and available to everyone for free.

Phase Six – Democratisation

At the inauguration of the Pope Benedict XVI in 2005, photos show a sea of heads staring towards the activity in front of them. Pictures of the inauguration of Pope Francis in 2013 show a stark difference. Instead of a sea of heads, it's a sea of devices. Almost every person present is photographing or filming the historic event on a smartphone or tablet. It's a picture that encapsulates the huge shifts for our society better than that single shot, and that happened in just eight short years.

Society is Going Digital

What we also see is that our complete society is digitised as well. Just like an image that is digitised in separate pixels, we humans are also becoming like separate pixels. Each one of us is one part of a bigger picture. Each individual has a mobile device that generates a trace of information, and that information is also like some kind of pixel that's digitised in the bigger picture. It's called big data, and the patterns of our collective behaviour can be mapped, catalogued, tracked and predicted using the information it gives us. Have you heard how the big technology companies use cookies to track what we do? The latest update to cookie technology is the use of a tiny image file, just one single pixel (an image too small to see). With millions of those pixels being opened on screens everywhere, if you think about it, all of those pixels represent a person who has looked at something online. We ourselves are being digitised by the advertisers already! A human decision, an action, a choice to look at something is represented by a piece of code. Our choices are catalogued, analysed, and our behaviour tracked already.

What we see happening at this moment is that extremely powerful technology will soon become very cheap (advertising costs have reduced to the extent where the perfect audience for your product gives you the ability to reach customers that only big corporate could afford just five years ago). Even by today's standards, technology is going to become so abundant it will be in the hands of billions of people. Technologies like artificial intelligence will very soon be available for almost all ordinary people.

Cheap communication technology and even virtually free energy generation won't be the preserve of the few; it will be available to everyone. Things that, only a few years ago, were only available to scientists, industry or large corporations will be freely available to us all.

Technology like robotics, drones, 3D and 4D printing, smart sensors, holographic computing and some ideas that haven't reached the market yet will be available to most people on the planet very soon (and some of those listed are already within reach of many of us right now).

The human race is already well into Phase One – Digitisation. To see where we could be going next, both in technology and human terms, it's essential to understand the patterns that drive progression.

Chapter 9

Predicting the Tsunami

As you have already seen, progression doesn't happen in a linear way. It happens through bursts of problems, solutions, and innovations. Change happens in waves.

We have a lot of warning signs that we can use to predict when a wave is coming and where it will appear. How you deal with the wave doesn't depend on the wave; it depends on the craft you are in at the time. Huge companies are like big ships as their size helps them to deal with most heavy weather – that's until something really big and unexpected comes over the horizon, and their size makes them slow to turn and difficult to manoeuvre. It doesn't help that the ship's crew (or company staff and management) knows just what a massive operation it is to change course. When you're big, it's easy and more comfortable to think that your size will protect you and that you can just secure the cargo (your existing products, services, and revenue streams) and keep steaming along in the same direction. After all, you're big. You can weather most storms.

But when a truly massive wave comes towards you at great speed you don't stand a chance. Everything gets smashed up and your rudder can't turn you away from danger quickly enough. The result? Well, at best you'll be left bobbing about, wondering how long it is before you're going to sink. At worst, the wave obliterates your ship (or company) before you even know what has happened.

Now, compare that to a single surfer. No baggage, quick reactions, and an instinct for the environment. After all, when you are so small compared to the sea, with so little to protect you, you learn to develop almost a sixth sense for everything going on around you. You pay attention.

A surfer doesn't try and plough through the wave, but they don't ignore it either. Surfers take in information from all their senses. They are quick to react, and the best riders almost have the sixth sense about when to ride the big wave and when to get out of the water.

To survive what's coming it's a good idea to be more like the surfer than the poor crew on the lumbering big ship. You want to be able to see the waves coming, don't you?

The size of the waves of change coming and the speed that they are building, as you are going to find out, means that it's wise to be on the surfboard, and not in the boat.

So what do you need to look out for? What are the signs that the weather is about to change? Well, it's already changed, you just can't see the systems building yet.

In technology and business, there are six stages of disruption. Let's summarise.

The first sign is that some kind of information is digitised and then it starts on a path of evolution that becomes unstoppable. Just like a tsunami. The disruption starts to obey Moore's law. That's when Phase One has started. But before we can make sense of what that really means let's take a look at the effect that has on the consumer and the market for your industry. How we buy and consume things is about to change forever. We are coming into The Super Power Consumer and The Age of the Entrepreneur, and you need to be ready. Your own financial survival depends on it.

Chapter10

The Super Power Consumer

Those exponential technology developments give consumers superpowers. It wasn't long ago that you would have to have been a company with very deep pockets, or a government agency with a ton of money to spend on research or to buy very expensive technology to do some things, but now those technologies are in the cloud, available for everyone, so everyone can do amazing things. It's not just start-ups either. Growth can happen at record rates. Take the growth of the cloud-based storage service Dropbox. They went from 400,000 users to over 4 million in just **fifteen months**.[5]

If someone has a bright idea in the morning, the person with the idea can fund it by the same evening by using a crowdfunding platform like Kickstarter, Fundable, or Indiegogo. The day after, that person can start production. Through the cloud, anyone can connect with a community of specialists; a great example is Quirky, the production community.

Quirky label themselves as an innovation platform. They have over 1.1 million members and have started over 293,000 inventions at the time of writing. It's a community where you can put your product idea in, then it will be curated to build a team of people with the perfect skills and the time to work on your project. Quirky is a community company whose mission is to make invention accessible. They state on their website: 'We believe everyone can be an inventor, and invention can happen anywhere.'

People are sourced and gathered for you: marketing people, engineers, packaging experts, people of a range of difference specialist skills and, after just thirteen weeks, it's viable that your product can go from idea to being on the shelves of the shops. Compare that to large corporations like Unilever. They need thirty **months** for the same process, so they have no

---

[5] source: http://theleanstartup.com/casestudies

chance to compete with these kinds of communities when it comes to speed of innovation and delivery. They are just too big and too slow at present.

The technology developments happening right now are so diverse, and will affect so many of our lives, that it can be difficult to comprehend. We are going to look into many developments that are in the early stages of the cycle in this book, but if I just listed many of them and gave you real examples, there's a good chance that so many of them would appear to be far-fetched, and these will be revealed in good time – in Part 2.

In the meantime, I'm going to do something that I believe you will find much more interesting. That is to look at the patterns that are driving both the developments themselves and the speed of those developments. That level of understanding will help you, your organisation, and your family to be much more adaptable and ready for what's coming next.

Chapter 11

The Age of the Entrepreneur

Just a few years ago, at the turn of 2000, it took at least $5 million of capital to start an internet company. By 2014, it cost less than $5,000 to start one.

That's a 99% cost reduction, and the cost of entry has dropped even further since then.

The cost barriers to internet innovation have virtually disappeared. Anyone with internet access can take a good idea and bring it to market. In the past, you had to develop the technology and own the equipment. Today, many services are available in the cloud on a pay-per-use basis, and that means you don't have to buy the technology anymore; you just rent it when you need it. That's a massive shift.

As a result, there's extreme decentralisation at the consumer level, so consumers are enabled and empowered to build a whole host of applications. If someone needs it and it doesn't exist yet, the person with the need can build it and make it a commercially viable proposition almost in a matter of hours with some basic skills.

The Apple App Store is a great example: in that one store alone there are more than 1.3 million different apps. Whatever your need, hobby, or problem, there's an app for it.

At the same time, we see back-end centralisation happening at a corporate level too. What I mean by that is that companies like Apple, Amazon, Microsoft, and Google are all building platforms that enable the consumer to leverage their proprietary technology. In fact, they provide many of the layers in the seven-layer model so that the consumer can leverage all the layers. From Apple allowing us all access to the App Store to sell the app we build at home, or the development kit to build an app, and the marketing tools and data storage tools from Amazon that are available for small businesses to rent at a cost of just a few cents a month. Giving us access to these shared platforms is empowering a lot of individuals. Microbusinesses have access to the tools of giants.

By the way, that behaviour and enabling of the small by the bigger structures is exactly the same as that which organ systems do inside our bodies. Organ systems empower individual cells to do more. It's now happening in the commercial world too, and later it's going to spread to other parts of our society too.

Going forward, I believe you will see an acceleration of large corporations being disrupted by communities of highly motivated, smart individuals.

Let's revisit Kodak again. In 1996, Kodak was a behemoth of a company with 28 billion market capitalisation and over 140,000 employees. In 2012, they were broke. They still had 17,000 employees, but in the very same year that Kodak filed for Chapter 11 bankruptcy protection, Facebook bought Instagram for $1 billion, and they only had thirteen people.

T-H-I-R-T-E-E-N people. Yes, you read that right. Old company with huge debts and outdated technology in the imaging space with its stock down the toilet versus a new company with just thirteen bright young people riding the wave worth a billion dollars.

The next wave will bring many companies head-to-head with the power of communities.

If we learn the lessons that the S-curve gives us, we see that people are extrinsically motivated in our current way of working (mostly – change is already happening). As we stand today, the main model is that most people get money to be there from nine to five and to do specific things. In traditional companies most employees are extrinsically motivated. Communities don't get money for doing the work – at least not directly. With participation in a community it's different. You are there because you like it, and you do something for a bigger purpose. We already have examples that have shown the power of people doing things for the greater good that they get intrinsic rewards for. Wikipedia is a great example; it's voluntary and unpaid, yet people update it and add to it every day. Open-source software is the same idea, and that's been around for a very long time now, with platforms like Linux where everything is open-source.

Eventually, when a product is produced through the power of a community, you share the benefits from it. **You get a fair share**.

Companies will have a hard time competing with those smart communities. They are now unstoppable and are springing up all over the place and they are enabled by smart software and network solutions.

If you compare that to our organisms or our body, the cells in our body don't get paid either, but they do get some kind of basic income. They do their work and in return they get food, shelter, warmth, but they don't get paid because they do what they are there to do – and want to do. People add stuff to Wikipedia because they have knowledge about things that interest them and they want to share it with others for its own sake. Information won't be trapped; it wants to expand and perpetuate itself and we are simply breathing vehicles for that.

We are a scaled-up version of what nature created on a cellular level. Our lung cells want to extract oxygen out of the air, and our heart cells want to beat.

This gives us a powerful indication of where humanity is also likely to go, given a choice. That choice already exists for many, even if most people don't realise it yet, and some are already walking down that path.

People will chase **their purpose** and will do what they like to do, and they will get a fair share of the benefits of doing it.

When you think of many of the great entrepreneurs, scientists, writers, technologists, artists, thinkers, inventors and creative people, we talk about their 'drive'. They are labelled as visionaries because they have refused to follow the conventional path and chosen instead to follow their purpose. They have something inside them that is so strong they can't NOT follow it.

Technology is giving more and more people that choice and already more and more people are taking it. The road less travelled is becoming travelled more frequently. What's interesting is that it means human diversity and specialist skills are developing more and more branches. Our expertise and experiences are also following an evolutionary S-curve as our technology allows us to share our purpose, share our vision and get other likeminded people on board with our ideas and vision.

Big companies will struggle unless they find a way to give a new generation of workers the sense of purpose they crave. If they don't provide it, an entrepreneurial community ready and waiting on a device in your pocket will provide it instead.

We are moving to a purpose-driven revolution – and nothing can stop progress.

Big change is coming.

Is your company ready?

Are you?

Chapter 12

The Spooky Secrets of the Super Power Curve

Nature is a beautiful thing. For all its diversity, nature follows simple patterns that are the result of simple physics and mathematics. That means that, despite the appearance of complexity, things are often simpler than they seem when you look in the right places and ask the right questions.

When you plot long-term development or progress on a graph for almost anything, you will see that the same pattern emerges time and time again. That pattern is a curve that elegantly describes an S shape.

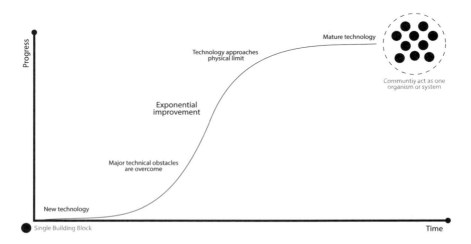

Figure 2: S-curve

Inside that S-curve there are seven key phases or waves of development, and inside each of those waves there is a series of seven smaller waves. Each wave starts slowly and gains momentum, and as it matures the next wave builds from it. At first the gains are small, slow, and easily missed; a classic factor in a lot of research and development is that everything looks small at first. But as the big problems along the curve get solved things start to speed up exponentially. When survival is assured, infrastructure gets built. When things can get moved around, we need more information about what is needed where. When we have that in place we need to automate some processes and after that, progress gets faster and faster. There comes a point where as the technology matures the speed of innovation slows down again because most of the key problems have been solved. Exactly the same happens in biology. Nature has the same patterns.

I was looking for patterns when I was doing my research into health. After all, as an AI and disruptive innovation specialist and someone who gets paid to look for patterns for companies so they can disrupt and innovate, I guess I started with an advantage. I was still surprised by the patterns that jumped out in front of me when I started to ask the right questions.

There are many recurring patterns in nature. Many of them follow the famous 'golden ratio' discovered by Fibonacci, for example the repeating patterns of leaves, the patterns of cauliflowers, the spirals of snails, ferns, and the growth patterns of corals. They are all around us and magnification of images has helped us see the wonders of how nature repeats and evolves itself. I realised that if I had a deeper understanding of how nature develops and evolves I was likely to gain greater insights into the next layer of our future.

I had a gut feeling that the clues to what was going to happen next were locked in those patterns somewhere.

My instincts told me that technology and where it's going had so much in common with how nature evolves that I was going to gain a deeper understanding.

I had always been fascinated by technology, and now with the burning need to understand how things worked to help my daughter, I knew there were new discoveries that could likely help her if I could see the patterns and break away from the straightjacket of institutional thinking.

It didn't take long to see that one of the most revealing patterns of all is the pattern of development itself. It's the very pattern that helps us to see how the next wave of change is going to impact us, and that pattern is called the S-curve.

Before I reveal the deep impact of the S-curve, and why getting your mind around the concept is so helpful in being able to predict what's coming next, it's vital to understand just how spooky and powerful this pattern really is in terms of using it as a predictive glimpse into the future.

When you see just how the S-curve runs through almost everything in our existence, it's possible to get how its power can be used to anticipate what's coming next and how it really is taking us towards a more sustainable world; a world of Humanification.

So let's take a short visit into a world that's truly freaky. A world of fractals. A world of parallels. A world where Quantum Innovation and the resulting Humanification of our technology becomes inevitable. You probably know that in the odd world of quantum physics, a particle can be in more than one place at the same time, allowing the parallel development of things. Parallel processing, if you like. And if you aren't familiar with the idea of parallel processing, it's simply when one problem is being solved in more than one way and in more than one place at the same time. That's exactly what's happening with our joined-up technology. It's pushing through a massive increase in speed of innovation and it's one of the contributing factors of the next big disruptive wave of change. We no longer need a single powerful computer in one institution. Instead we have millions of people and their computers solving complex technical challenges all at the same time. It's bringing wave after wave of new ideas and fresh thinking. The S-curve pattern is all around us and it's transforming our world. From the smallest cell to the most complex technology, the pattern and the waves are present.

I discovered that everything, from a single cell through to your own physical body of 10 trillion cells, all the plants, all the animals on the planet, AND our technology, and even artificial intelligence have followed an almost identical pattern of development. Everything follows the pattern of the S-curve. There are even those seven S-curves within each big S-curve.

Each part of the curve has that seven-wave pattern within it. It's like a fractal: patterns within patterns within patterns. The curve repeats from atoms upwards. Did you know that sub-atomic particles form atoms with seven layers of electrons orbiting the nucleus? That the periodic system has seven families? That atoms form more molecular structures following the S-curve pattern? That those complex molecules form DNA and transition to prokaryote cells, to eukaryote cells, and that human and our societies' structures ALL follow the same pattern of development?

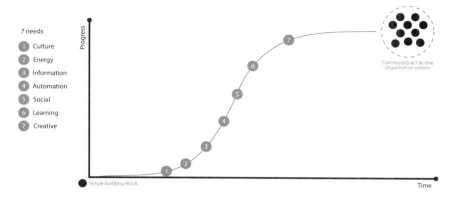

Figure 3: The Seven Needs inside every S-curve

This incredible repeating patterns of life gives us more than a glimpse into our future. It also shows that what's going to happen next is going to happen much faster than we probably think, and I'm going to share the hidden secrets of why that is.

To do that, we need to first step into a time machine to get a new perspective on the building blocks of evolution and innovation. It might sound incredible, but:

- All organic life develops along the S-curve
- Humans interact and organise themselves along the S-curve
- Technology develops along the S-curve

All three follow the very same patterns. It's a triad and a blueprint for the future: biology, technology, humanity. They all follow the pattern of the S-curve, a magical triad all following the same pattern.

It's a pattern that gives us predictive powers, allows us to understand what's missing, and enables us to see what gaps we need to fill next. In turn, that will help us make the progress humanity needs to make to take us to the next level; significantly, it also helps us to predict and build the next generation of business models.

This strange triad of technology, biology, and humanity is more connected than it might at first appear. So now let's take a deeper look at what's really going on by grasping the amazing power of this subtle but amazing little pattern; a pattern that affects the lives of every single one of us. In fact, it's going on inside your own body right now – and by understanding it you may gain a greater understanding of how to stay healthy yourself. Wouldn't that be a bonus? Not only will you have an idea of how the world is going to change, but you will also give yourself a longer period on the planet to play a part in it.

The Ultimate Expression of Change

So let's take a look at how this S-curve expresses itself and how it helps us to anticipate the next waves that are likely to come over the horizon so you can ride the wave instead of one of the unfortunate people in the capsizing boat. Remember, if you can save yourself, you can help others . . .

When you can see the pattern and know how to apply it to whatever business or situation you are in, you can make 'educated guesses' about what's likely to develop in the next phase.

You are able to almost look into a crystal ball, but to do that, you need to be able to do several things:

- Understand what part of the technology curve we are in now
- Identify whether the foundations that the next part of the curve grow from have been built yet – or not
- Have an indication of the current speed of change (I can help you with that one!)
- Know what to look for in the current environment that signals the next wave of innovation is happening or about to happen
- What happens in the next 'layer' of change in the next part of the curve

The Super Seven

There are seven core waves of development and innovation. Each phase sub-divides the S-curve into distinct sections, or layers, where predictable things happen as you travel along and up the curve and through each layer.

These phases (or layers, if you prefer) are like imaginary *steps* up through the levels of the curve, and they give us the opportunity to assess where we are now, and to anticipate what's coming next – and ultimately where the development has the potential to take our technology. We can also, to a certain extent, predict the impact of the innovation if we are open-minded enough.

By understanding the S-curve and the distinct layers within it, we can see what's missing at each level and speed up innovation by filling in the gaps if the technology already exists to do it. Each wave creates a launch pad for the next wave to build on.

If the technology that lays the foundation for the next layer doesn't exist yet, at least we know what we have to do next, in order to move forward and upwards with the innovation.

Understanding the S-curve is key to grasping the next wave coming over the horizon.

In evolution or creation we see the same S-curve process repeating over and over again. So let's start by illustrating how **biology** follows the S-curve, and then we can make comparisons and extrapolations from there. As you will see later on, you will be able to use the curve to identify where you, your organisation, or your product or service sit on the curve. That will enable you to see what the next evolutionary layer is and whether things have a way to go to get there, or if disruption is just around the corner.

Cycles are shorter and shorter and go exponentially faster and each wave has a deeper impact because it upgrades all the layers below.

Chapter 13

S-curve in a Nutshell

So let's summarise the essential concept of the S-curve and why it matters so much. After that we can move on to seeing the context of the S-curve and using its incredible predictive power.

Now you know that there are seven disruptive stages inside each major wave of disruptive innovation in the natural world. You also know that there are seven disruptive waves inside each major wave of technology innovation too. Both waves have the same characteristics and follow the same pattern for one simple reason: both disruptive waves are solving the same problems. It doesn't matter if the problems are on a leaf or a silicon chip; ultimately both must solve the same challenges to grow, thrive, and move on to the next phase.

You've discovered that each big S-curve contains a series of seven little S-curves inside it, in much the same way that a fern or snail shell contains lots of repeating patterns inside that show the same overall pattern in miniature. You found out that one full S-curve has seven little curves inside it, and each little curve follows the same S-curve pattern in miniature.

You know why every big wave of technology innovation behaves in the same way as an S-curve behaves in nature. You also know that every mini-wave phase of the disruptive journey starts slowly, gains momentum, and reaches maturity and serves as a foundation for the next mini-wave above it to build upon. The first part of the S-curve starts with lots of research and development without much (apparently) to show for it. Somewhere, one of those pieces of R&D solves one of the problems inside the **survival** mini-curve, then an **infrastructure** mini-curve problem is solved, then the **information** mini-curve challenge gets sorted out, and the **automation** mini-curve can start. In technology terms, I believe that we are now halfway up the inside a huge disruptive wave and everything is speeding up exponentially because we are at the exponential part of the curve.

The next stage inside the big S-curve is that the technology (or biology, if we are looking at Nature's patterns) matures and the speed of innovation then slows down because most of the problems have been solved.

Eventually, the technology is fully mature and the new 'organism' has a type of collective consciousness that helps it operate as a single functional being.

That's where we are going with our ever more connected world, and there are going to be some big surprises. Surprises that are going to land on your doorstep and in your workplace faster than you think.

The S-curve pattern, and understanding it, can help us to predict and prepare for some huge disruptions that are coming as a result of our technology developing at the exponential rate that it is at this point in our history.

Our ever more interconnected world and our ability to talk to each other and share ideas is going to change everything. It's going to change how we share our wealth, how we exchange value, how we power our world, grow our food, manage our waste, produce the products we need, share resources, and distribute them to those who need them.

Many of our old institutions and established companies are going to crumble and the fight to hold on to the old is going to become more and more of a losing battle for many people.

Those of us who are ready to embrace change and enjoy the challenges ahead are going to be able to help the others.

By revealing the patterns of nature and how we can disrupt things in a healthy way, and growing our trust in Nature's ability to solve problems without total self-destruction, I believe we can move forward in a way that is good for all of us.

So the next big question is this. If we are on a technology S-curve, where are we at the moment? And what's going to happen next?

Chapter 14

What part of the Tech Curve are we in now?

Whether you are a manager, an entrepreneur, a business owner, or a board member, understanding what part of the disruption curve your business or sector is in right now gives you a serious edge. Think of it like some kind of early warning system for disruptive change that's about to hit your business. Also, by understanding where you are now, you have the potential to innovate and generate new opportunities.

It's going to really help you to ask and answer three key questions.

Am I at the beginning of the S-curve?

Am I at the exponential part of the S-curve (where you can earn a lot of money, accumulate a lot of influence)?

Am I on the maturity part of the S-curve, where the layer is almost fully automated? If you are here, then there's almost certainly no more market share for you to gain.

Although we aren't always aware of it, almost our every action is powered by information technology.

Not long before I started writing this, the new iPad Pro launched, and it looks and feels like a piece of paper!

You can write on it, and it feels like an analogue thing, not a digital thing. More and more technology feels more and more natural, to the point where we don't even think of it as technology anymore.

In 1981, a GPS receiver device cost more than 110,000 euros, and it weighed 24 kilos.

Now, a similar chip costs only five euros, weighs almost nothing, and it is very, very accurate. It can give you precision in 3D locations within ten centimetres accuracy. By the time this book goes to print, those numbers will have almost certainly changed again.

Another example is the memory chip for your digital photography, taken with your smartphone. Within nine years, the amount of storage has improved, yet the price has almost stayed the same.

Products where digital information is involved or digital processing is involved are exponentially better, cheaper, and smaller.

Technology obeys the S-curve.

The next generation of technology is already there. We already have computers that work with photons and ions instead of electrons. They can put the same processing power currently only available commercially in a complete data centre and give you the same power and storage in a space that would fit in the palm of your hand.

Google have even claimed that their new quantum computers are one hundred million times faster than today's machines.

It is going fast, very fast. Even Moore's law itself is already outdated. We now have Rose's law. Rose's law is a doubling of Moore's law, so it's quadrupling every twelve to eighteen months.

So what does this all mean? okay, it's time to find out.

Part 2
The 7 Waves of Innovation

Chapter 15

Overview – So where is the Future taking Us?

The Secrets are Hidden Inside The Waves

We live in a universe of movement, patterns, and repeating cycles. Being able to see the waves that drive our world has always been a very in-demand skill. Thankfully, seeing what's coming is no longer the preserve of 'visionaries'. With an understanding of the patterns of change, you can see what's coming too. Even better, you can be a key part of it.

Big data and the rise of technology allow us all to take our collective knowledge, extrapolate the data, and glimpse the future. To do that, you simply need to realise and relax into the understanding that **everything** moves in waves.

- History moves in waves
- Technology moves in waves
- Energy moves in waves
- Sound moves in waves
- The financial markets move in waves.

Almost everything moves in waves. But here's the thing about waves: when one wave solves one problem and reaches a peak, the fact that that very wave existed in the first place now creates the conditions for the next problem to exist. Each wave creates a platform to launch the next wave. Each new wave leverages the power of the previous wave. That is why everything is going faster and faster. In the same way that a rocket is made out of multiple parts, every part of the rocket that's ignited gives the entire rocket more speed and builds upon the speed it already had.

That's the repeating pattern of the development of everything. With that knowledge and understanding we can start to see where things are going in the future. That future may be simply the little changes in your home or the bigger impact of global changes. The pattern applies in diverse situations going from wearable technology right through to the future of our energy use, and even to the usefulness and nature of governments.

Many of the changes that confuse people suddenly become clear when you have a way of seeing where you are now. Context is everything. Being able to recognise which wave of development you are in, and what the characteristics of the next wave are likely to be, has always been (and will always be) a highly prized commodity. Giving you that special skill of being able to see what makes each type of wave so unique is what this section of this book is all about.

Sometimes, some of the concepts might not appear to be connected at first. Sometimes, you might even think the developments, technologies, and human drivers have connections that appear tenuous at best. But here's the thing: there are no accidents in Nature; instead, there are predicable forces and motivations *when you know where to look.*

It's often only when you stand back far enough and look at the bigger picture and the patterns that everything starts to make sense. So that's what we are going to do together. We are going to take a tour through the 7 Waves of Innovation and start to bring together some of the things that are happening in the world of technology, some of the big issues facing the human race, our communities, our planet, and swirl all that together with the core needs that drive each of us to do what we do and why we do it. Out of that mass of facts and ideas you will see the patterns emerge for yourself, meaning you will be better equipped than ever and give yourself a head start in getting ready for a future that's coming at us faster than ever. In addition, it may well provide the creative spark in you, so you could be at the forefront of a new innovation that will change the world.

If you can't see the connections each time, that's okay. By the time you start to see the bigger picture it will all make sense and you will be significantly better prepared for what's coming than many of your peers.

Problems and Solutions come in waves

Each wave of expansion that happens in almost any field, including Nature, human development, or technology (and as you are starting to see by now – those three things have more in common than you probably first thought), creates a massive potential for new growth. That growth creates a new challenge to be overcome, and the growth that arises from that solution creates another problem!

It's a never-ending cycle of problem, solve the problem, create a problem, and solve a problem.

It happens in Companies

Take the example of a company. All companies and businesses follow a similar and predictable cycle, yet over and over again it fails to be recognised by people who are too close to it to be able to see it. Every stage of business growth, and every corporate expansion, creates wave after wave of new problems and a series of new challenges that need to be solved. As one wave of business growth reaches new heights, it creates another new problem that needs to be solved and the cycle starts over again.

For example, as the number of people in a business grows, you see the need for more leadership. More staff need more leaders, and leaders need meetings to transfer requirements to the people in the business. Then, all those meetings need people to organise them and managers to manage the organisers! It's a cycle. And it always comes in waves. When you have more customers and more orders you need more staff or inventory to fulfil orders, and when you have more staff and inventory, you create a need for more marketing so that new costs can be met next month and next year. You get the idea. One success always leads to new challenges appearing.

Progress always happens in waves.

In human terms, it's quite understandable why we often only see the waves when they get pretty close to the shore. That's because, as a species, we tend to only solve problems when they become acute. We don't have time to do much else, and we don't really need to most of the time either.

Think about it, do you regularly go and check the tyres of your car for nails and stones or do you just react when you get a flat tyre? We only tend to notice problems when they become painful. A stone in your tyre might lead to a problem in a few days' or weeks' time, but it doesn't cause any grief so it's not worth thinking about until it does. That's how most people live their lives; in reactive mode.

Yet, when we think we are about to get taken out by some potential impending disaster, we do something about it – or at least talk about it with our friends. The imagined disaster scenario is what the media thrives on. In other words, when our problems get really painful, we deal with them effectively. Before that, we just speculate for the variety and entertainment value of it but do precious little else to change things.

So back to the business scenario. In a company, when people get overworked, we take on more staff, but not before things have usually got pretty uncomfortable for a while first. Instinctively we know that more staff might ease the problem, but it inevitably leads to a new set of problems.

In this section what I want to help you to see is what the unique nature of each wave looks like, and which wave some of our core institutions, utilities, and some of the big issues that affect our day-to-day life are in right now. That will help you to make sense of some of the developments that are happening right now and be a little less shocked when the next ones happen.

If you are standing on a beach, and there's a tsunami coming, it really helps if you are looking out to sea with some glasses on, not looking back at the land and hoping you are going to stay safe.

Chapter 16

So What Drives Us?

The Story of The Driven Human

Back in 1943, Abraham Maslow, a renowned academic and psychologist, published a paper called 'A Theory of Human Motivation'.[6] Inside this remarkable paper, Maslow documented a groundbreaking piece of thinking about what really drives us. He asked the key question: what do people need and want, and why? His answers to those fundamental questions became the now famous 'Maslow's Pyramid'.

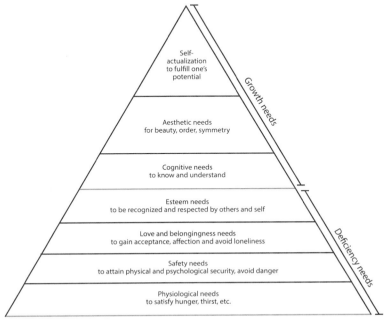

Figure 4: Maslow's Pyramid

---

[6] https://en.wikipedia.org/wiki/Maslow%27s_hierarchy_of_needs

It's an elegant model that describes our human needs, what drives us, and the order (oh yes, there's a natural order there too) in which we naturally try to satisfy our needs. Like all good waves, the achievement or meeting of one need creates the conditions for the next need to exist. In today's interpretation of the pyramid there are just five layers, but originally, there were seven (just like there are 7 Waves of Humanification ...).

Cycles frequently occur in patterns of seven layers, seven waves, or seven repetitions. It's a force of Nature.

Whether you look at human needs, the drivers of biology, or the phases that technology goes through, there are seven stages, waves, or levels in almost ALL developmental processes. And each process goes through cycles that repeat at some systematic level. We are going to come back to this model many more times during the course of this book, so it's worth spending a moment having a good look at it and doing your own thinking about how it relates to your world.

That's the beauty of our universe, our world, and ourselves. When you know where to look there are predictable patterns, and yet those same patterns create almost infinite variety. The variety is what keeps life exciting, yet the predictable patterns are still there and they give us a virtual telescope we can use to look into the future when we try and work out where our technology and humanity is going.

It's the infinite variety around the edges of each wave, and the unique way of adapting at each stage of development of a technology, that feeds the amazing diversity and creativity that takes us forward as a species. The patterns apply to everything around us. The patterns drive diversity and depth. They bring richness and interest to every idea because everything has the opportunity to divide, cluster, and become more complex. Even a simple idea has pros and cons. One simple idea can soon double, and double again.

The beauty of the never-ending cycle of waves is this. As we move up from one wave to the next, we can solve bigger and bigger problems each time. But despite the diversity, the core patterns are always still there; they are like a hidden blueprint driving everything we do and everything that happens to us. It's the same hidden blueprint that drives biology, drives us, and it drives technology innovation too. Increasingly you are going to start to see the patterns of the human needs that Maslow identified mapping across to the technology developments, the same patterns that Nature can help us to predict. We have so many ways to see where things are going and that's almost the problem. We don't know where to look because there is too much information. But when you have a prism that starts to concentrate the patterns into visible themes, doors start to open. When you bring all these ideas from human behaviour, Nature, and technology together, magic starts to happen.

So let's start to look about how these three ideas of human needs, biology, and technology start to weave together. Being able to see how they interact will help you see what's coming over the horizon and predict the future in your field of expertise.

Humanification Wave 1.0 – The Survival Wave

Wave 1.0 exists and is driven by the same core needs. So whether you are referring to the

- lowest layer on Maslow's pyramid,
- first phase of evolutionary biology,
- first wave of a new technology development
- creation of any first generation of a cultural system,

it's inside Wave 1.0 that you realise that EVERY system is always dealing with a primary survival need that's common across everything. Phase One of Wave 1.0 takes care of these primary survival needs. In Wave 1.0 **people** need to meet our most basic needs of self-preservation (food, water, shelter, sleep, clothing, finding a mate). This is what causes us to cluster together. All our basic needs are more easily met inside a bigger community. That leads to the start of the next phase of Wave 1.0, which is the development of towns, cities, nations, unions, online communities – in other words, any other structures where bigger groups increase our chances of success.

It's for basic survival reasons that cells have the exact same qualities. In Phase Two of Wave 1.0, cells group together to survive too. So in all first waves, things simply replicate (Phase One) and then cluster (Phase Two). People group together in first waves; cosmic dust pulls together and, when it gets into big enough clumps, starts to feel the pull of gravity at an ever-increasing rate. In summary, everything that happens in first waves is based on things pulling together into groups to increase the chance of survival and success. There's a whole chapter coming up, where we will be looking at some examples of first waves and how to spot them building.

Every time you recognise something that's in a Wave 1.0 phase of development you have an opportunity to use it to innovate by taking it to the next wave – and that's Wave 2.0.

Humanification Wave 2.0 – The Security and Communication Wave

In Wave 2.0 everything centres around security. It maps to the second layer of Maslow's pyramid, the second stage of the biology cycle (which is the infrastructure phase, where things start to connect and form networks that keep the organism safe and functional), and to the second level of technology innovation, where we see things growing big enough to need communications systems. So you can see that Wave 2.0 always connects back to the same core needs and functions: safety and security.

It's in Wave 2.0 where useful infrastructures start to be built. Wave 2.0 people seek to look after our health, provide employment, and seek and offer protection (social security systems, steady jobs, government welfare, and family support systems for example). The whole idea of 'society' exists as an expression of our safety need. 'There's safety in numbers', as they say … But as soon as something starts to grow there's always a need for some sort of framework. For example, for society to work effectively we need rules and laws that protect us from anger and violence. People need order, law, and stability to be able to collaborate, because society just doesn't work without clear rules of engagement.

Humanification Wave 3.0 – The Connection Wave

You could call the third wave of the Humanification model the communication wave. When you look at the third level of the needs pyramid that Maslow talks about, you see that he refers to our deep human need for belonging, love, and connection. Those things are the heart of our third-layer needs.

In technology terms, this human need for connection was expressed, and met, by the birth of the telecommunication revolution. People want to connect to each other over long distances. It's in our nature to want to connect with family and friends; to be able to pass on gossip and wisdom and enjoy the connection and affection with our fellow humans. The telecoms revolution allowed that to become a reality and in the process changed the face of business and industry too.

It's natural for us to want to connect with each other not only when we're in the same neighbourhood, but also over a long distance. Telecommunication makes that possible. The telephone and the smartphone are the ultimate definition of connecting to family and friends and, more recently, video is starting to take over, with Skype and Apple's FaceTime becoming as useful, if not more, than voice calling alone. It's becoming a highly competitive space with Google Hangouts (which was always powered by YouTube live streaming technology) and Facebook's Live function all trying to grab a big market share of the live communication market.

Humanification Wave 4.0 – The Automation to Emotion Wave

Wave 4.0 is all about automation that creates room for emotion.

In biology, there's a huge amount of automation. For example, we can breathe without thinking about it. Taking a breath is a fully automated process. The body and cells start to work more automatically and this allows our needs to be met in more sophisticated ways. Think of our human hardware being robust enough to start running more sophisticated software and you'll understand how automation leads to our 4.0 need for things beyond mere 1.0 survival, 2.0 security, and 3.0 connection. In Wave 4.0 we need good feelings to function.

The fourth layer in Maslow's pyramid refers to 'esteem' needs. This is where autonomy (our ability to make our own independent choices) becomes of key importance to people. In Wave 4.0 we start to be driven less by our physical needs and start looking for things that bolster how we feel and relate to each other. Wave 4.0 needs include more sophisticated concepts like achievement, status, responsibility, reputation, self-acceptance; these are the things that are driving in this layer of revolution.

You also see that most of the economy is still in this layer. You can tell because our status and reputation is very important. It's the old economy, if you will, from the nineties, eighties and seventies.

When your 1.0 survival needs, your 2.0 security needs, your 3.0 connection needs have been met, then you can start to get more picky about how you want things in your life to be. Things that are the most emotional in nature start to become the things that are really important.

Humanification 5.0 – The Social Wave

In Wave 5.0 people want to gather knowledge, meaning, self-awareness, self-expression, and that's what you see happen on the big sharing platforms like Twitter, Facebook, YouTube, but also the asset-sharing platforms. Humans and technology are starting to merge here. The platforms and the people are becoming indistinguishable. It's all possible because of the technological developments that came before.

I believe that in the developed countries we are in Wave 5.0 right now. In some Third World countries, large swathes of the population are still in survival mode and are in Wave 1.0 or 2.0. With the advent of some of the new technologies coming on stream we will be able to help those countries catch up with the rest of us.

Humanification Wave 6.0 – The Artistry Layer

If we go to the next layer, we move from social platforms to true learning platforms. It's a bit like the neocortex layer of our own evolution. It only came into being when everything was in place from Waves 1.0 to 5.0 in biological terms. In Wave 6.0 of cycles we see that aesthetic needs like beauty, balance, form, and self-reflection are the main drivers.

That is what we do exactly at this moment with machine learning algorithms. They are helping us to attempt to design more beautiful products, more balanced communities, more balanced solutions or processes within companies. Form will be redefined by these learning platforms. I call them learning platforms because they won't just be learning from us, they will be learning from their own learning. This could be called the first true AI layer. Here, machines will also be able self-reflect, learn things about themselves, about our community, and give us the feedback or the reflection to adjust our progress in the right direction.

Humanification Wave 7.0 – Higher Purpose

Finally, you have the creation, or co-creation, platforms layer. In this layer, self-actualisation and transcendence are the main drivers according to Maslow's hierarchy of needs. This is where we need personal growth, morality, fulfilment, where we place others' needs above self, and where we focus on our own self-knowledge. We already see this happening all around us, though in my view we haven't really developed this yet to a significant level. For example, it's already the case that people have an expectation that commercial companies also fulfil a duty to a certain level of morality within our society. People are also seeking ever greater fulfilment from within, developed through their own jobs and their work. That is where we are going. The jobs that we hate but currently do for the money won't be there in the future; they'll be done by robots and artificial intelligence.

We will do work that is fulfilling and helps our society to a higher level. What's interesting is that the millennial generation are heading firmly on a course in this direction already. If you are hiring young people, you are going to need to make sure that they believe that they are doing something worthwhile. We have moved into the conscience generation and I predict that the need for the millennial generation to have a positive influence and do meaningful work will make a fundamental difference to our world.

So how is this relevant to technology? How do the seven human needs help us map and predict where technology is going to take us? Well, if the waves of innovation are going to be useful to you – if you are going to be able to relate them to your own industry, business, or career – it helps to have a deeper understanding so you can transfer the theories on to your own situation. So let's look at another intriguing connection, and that is how those seven needs have a direct relationship with what happens in biology.

The 7 Waves – Nature's Map

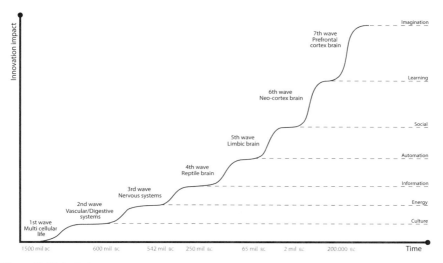

Figure 5: Biological waves

These seven technological waves mapped to Nature may sound a bit odd, but it helps us to understand that these waves are part of a pattern that started long before people (and even the first single-cell organisms that were here long before us) inhabited the earth. The biology behind much of the technology we are going to talk about later makes much more sense when you start to spot the connections.

Here are some fascinating examples of how the waves play out in Nature and technology, so let's look at some examples to help make sense of the ideas so far.

Wave 1.0 – What Biology Did: Cell Communities

The first biological wave helped single-cell organisms to meet their basic needs. Cells started to develop some kind of communication and started to work together and formed multicellular culture and communities. These became organisms that were, in effect, using biotechnology to increase their survival rate. These single cells started to work together and form bigger structured communities, like coral reefs (shelter) to gather and filter food more efficiently (agriculture) from the ocean tides.

Wave 1.0 – What Technology Did: The Agricultural Revolution

Technological Wave 1.0 delivered technology that met our basic physiological and biological human needs. Technology like agriculture (food), buildings and towns (shelter/sleep), irrigation (water), fire (warmth), laws and government (homeostasis), and many more.

Wave 2.0 – What Biology Did: To Get Comfort and Safety

The second biological wave helped the cell communities (organisms) to meet their needs of safety and comfort. It helped the organisms to form a digestive system (industry) that processed food more efficiently and distributed nutrition (energy) through a vascular system (infrastructure). In this way an organism could distribute the energy more efficiently throughout the organism, which enabled it to thrive and grow even faster (health).

Wave 2.0 – What Technology Did: The Industrial Revolution

Technological Wave 2.0 delivered technology that met our needs for safety and comfort. Infrastructure technologies provided us with a stable environment to build nations: we were able to have employment (industrial infrastructure), reliable transportation systems (transport infrastructure), constant energy flow (pipeline and cable infrastructure for oil and electricity), pharmaceuticals (healthcare infrastructure), etc.

Wave 3.0 – What Biology Did: Love and Connection

The third biological wave helped the fast-growing cell communities (organisms) to meet their love and connection needs. The cell communities had grown rapidly and distances became bigger between separate parts of the cell community (organism). Cell communities started to form nerve networks that re-connect the outer parts of the community in real time so that they could work together even more efficiently (connection). Cell communities also started to develop senses that helped the community to create a better awareness of their surroundings.

Wave 3.0 – What Technology Did: The Telecom Revolution

Technological Wave 3.0 delivered us technology that met our needs to connect with each other. Telecommunication technology enabled real-time communication between family, our loved ones (meeting our love needs), and let us build and maintain relations over long distances (meeting our connection needs).

Wave 4.0 – What Biology Did: The Autonomy Needs of a Cell Community

The fourth biological wave helped the cell communities (organism) to meet the needs of self-esteem and autonomy. Cell communities (organisms) started to develop automated routines that helped them to automate internal processes and also helped them to hunt more efficiently. Cell communities developed an operating system (reptile brain) that was like a software layer upon all the biological hardware.

Wave 4.0 – What Technology Did: The Automation Revolution

Technological Wave 4.0 delivered new technology that meets our need for autonomy. Software technology such as operating systems and applications automated all kind of processes and routines for us. Software gave our technology almost instinctive behaviour that was 'programmed in' and made our technology much easier to manage.

Wave 5.0 – What Biology Did: Cognitive Needs of a Cell Community

The fifth biological wave helped the cell communities (organisms) to meet their cognitive needs. Cell communities developed a mammal brain technology that provided memory (knowledge), which helped organisms to remember specific environments, situations, and behaviours; it also gave the organism social skills (self-awareness and expression) that enabled them to share and copy successful behaviours from other mammals.

Wave 5.0 – What Technology Did: The Social Media Revolution

Technological Wave 5.0 delivered new technology that met our cognitive needs: technology such as search engines (our need for knowledge), social networks (our need for self-awareness and self-expression), and task-specific communities (our need for meaning).

Wave 6.0 – What Biology Did: The Aesthetic Needs of a Cell Community

The sixth biological wave helped cell communities to meet their aesthetic needs. Technology like the neocortex brain helped them to learn faster and solve more complex problems; it also gave rise to the first tools and drawings (beauty and form), it helped us to walk upright (balance), and it enabled the development of basic communication (self-reflection).

Wave 6.0 – What Technology Did: The AI Revolution

Technological Wave 6.0 holds the promise to deliver new technology that will help us to meet our aesthetic needs: technology like cloud-based neural networks that are able to learn and create almost perfect algorithms (to enhance beauty and form), robots that learn to walk and move like people (balance), and even the creation of advanced virtual agents who can help us with all kinds of processes (self-reflection).

Wave 7.0 – What Biology Did: Self-actualisation and Transcendence

The seventh biological wave helped cell communities to meet their needs of self-actualisation and transcendence. Technology like the prefrontal cortex enabled cell communities (organisms, including we humans) to improve themselves and develop advanced language and share concepts and ideas (personal growth and self-knowledge); it helped them to develop agriculture and civilisation (morality and place others' need above self), and it helped them to do things that gave them satisfaction (fulfilment and purpose).

Wave 7.0 – What Technology Is Going to Do: The Creative Revolution

Technological Wave 7.0 holds the promise to deliver us new technology that will meet our need for self-actualisation and transcendence. I think it's likely that we will see the advent of Digital Doubles (who will help us achieve faster personal growth, self-knowledge, and transcendence), hive minds, and decision-making platforms (that will help us with tough morality questions and give us a mechanism to place the needs of the many above the needs of self), and we will see more co-creation platforms (to help us reach fulfilment and help us serve our purpose).

Chapter 17

The 7 Technology Waves in a Nutshell

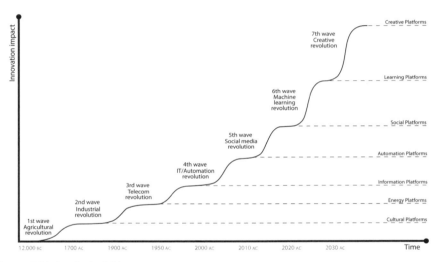

Figure 6: Technological Waves

There is a remarkable similarity in the patterns to the evolution of much of our human technology. The diagram shows how each of our major technology revolutions are related to the biological drivers that now appear obvious now you know what you know. Each new wave has provided us (and will provide us) with new technology that meets a higher human need. Increasing technology access will push humanity upwards towards a purpose-driven society full of happiness and fulfilment. We can, and will, be more 'human' in the future. The Humanification process will make jobs more suited to our needs, help our cities to be better designed, our governments to become more streamlined and democratic, our healthcare systems to be more efficient, our business, our products, and so many more things more human than ever before. Each new technology wave will push us upward and empower the individual even more. Each new wave will also upgrade the previous technology layers and, as a result, disrupt the existing technology, business, and power structures. Problems will continue to be solved much more efficiently, so the solutions that we had before will become obsolete because the problem they solved doesn't exist any more.

Chapter 18

The Mystery and Magic of Memory

'Patterns of information is memory.'
– William Brown, Research Scientist, RPF

I don't believe that evolution is as accidental as some people make it out to be. For me, there's a pattern to these accidents.

Just like biology follows patterns of development, technology follows a precise pattern of development too. As William Brown, quoted above, said, a pattern of information **is** memory.

Extend that idea slightly and it becomes easy to see that if a pattern repeats, it becomes predictable. Memory does have the capacity to help us predict the future. That key idea may just become the blueprint that enables you yourself to look into the future of technology. That's exactly what I'm hoping to help you do. Many people hear about these ideas in my talks and tell me that they come up with connection after connection and idea after idea after they hear the presentation. Over time I hope that more and more people will follow through with their ideas and collaborate with others and bring them to life (you can find out how to become part of the Humanification community at the end of this book).

A Vision for the Future

I believe that more and more human needs can, and will, be fulfilled by the increasing use of technology. Each wave that's automated or powered by technology helps us to better meet our needs on each and every level, and that in turn pushes humanity to a new level again.

For example, when we don't have to worry about fulfilling our basic human survival needs like food, shelter, water and sleep, we can focus on creating the next level of infrastructure that makes things more safe and comfortable. If eventually technology will help us fulfil all seven layers of our human needs, there will only be the top level of the pyramid to focus on – that means living a life of purpose. It gives me great optimism to think there is the chance of us becoming a society where personal growth, morality, fulfilment, purpose, self-knowledge, and placing the needs of others above self is where our human potential can take us.

At this moment technology is able to fulfil the first five layers of the needs of humanity (in developed countries at least). Thankfully, the exponential curve of progress is helping us move so fast, that better technology will soon be much cheaper and more readily available for more and more people. That development has the power to fulfil more and more needs for more and more people. It really can and will help many more people solve the dire problems that have held humanity back, giving more and more people the possibility to unlock the incredible potential locked up inside of every one of us. Add to that the potential for developing a collective intelligence, and I believe we will see miracles happen within the next disruptive wave that's building up right now.

In this section of the book I am going to look at each wave in turn. We are going to dive deeper into the mechanics and you are going to get some of your most important questions answered. I'll do my best to illuminate issues like:

- Where are we in the cycle?
- What are the drivers for the next new innovations?
- What are the trends telling us?
- What next-generation technology is gaining commercial traction?
- What are some of the longer-term implications?

Inevitably, some of the waves are subjective. Some of the trends don't fit neat and easy classifications. Some of the ideas have been around for a while and some of them are radical. What they all have in common is that they follow some kind of pattern. They all map to one or more of our key human needs and this helps us understand where the technology can take us. I hope you discover some ideas you haven't already heard about, identify some new connections that you haven't made before, and generally be inspired to join a growing global community of change-makers that will help to advance our world.

Chapter 19

Wave 1.0 – How will our Society Work in the Future?

The Rise of Virtual Government

At the end of 1991, following the breakup of the Soviet Union, a small group of government officials in a tiny little corner of what was, essentially, a brand new micro-country, got together round a table to solve a whole host of knotty but decidedly refreshing problems.

The challenges they faced are just like the challenges many small companies face today, the biggest one being this: how can a tiny player of a country, with only around 1 million people, survive and compete in a world dominated by 'big players'?

The country was Estonia, and the people found themselves in a rather unusual situation. Without suffering the consequences of a damaging war, they suddenly had the opportunity to build a government and a country from scratch. It was a Wave 1.0 chance of a lifetime.

The then Ambassador to the United States, Toomas Hendrik Ilves (who was later to become President of Estonia), realised that it was possible to use the internet to give the country more clout than its tiny size and rather out-of-the-way location would suggest.

It was a wise move. Within a few short years Estonia, or E-stonia as it was cleverly re-branded, had the largest number of start-up companies per capita in the world. It also decided to build some policies that were forward-looking in the extreme. For example, in Estonia, the internet is considered a human right and all residents have free wi-fi. They introduced a flat taxation system and import tariffs were scrapped. They put education and healthcare online faster than many (supposedly) wealthier economies managed to. In Estonia, you own your own data and all public expenditure is transparent and available online. Some amazing companies came out of Estonia because the conditions were brilliant for start-ups. For example, Skype may have been founded by a Dane and a Swede, but the software was created by three Estonians, Ahti Heinla, Priit Kasesalu, and Jaan Tallinn.

It became a hotbed for disruptive technology because of the environment that was created, giving entrepreneurs the space to exist in Estonia. A peer-to-peer structure was able to flourish after the Soviet breakdown that allowed citizens with dreams to connect to each other and circumvent the big banks and even create their own telecoms infrastructure.

Like all waves of change, it brought new problems. For example, Estonia is vulnerable to cyberattack because it's so dependent on the internet. In 2007 their networks were subject to a major cyber attack allegedly perpetrated by the Russians. But, as you know by now, one problem creates the opportunity for another solution. Estonia's young technologists reacted with groups of young cyber security experts volunteering for the Estonian army, and now NATO recognises Estonia as a 'cyber defence centre of excellence'.

So what can we learn from Estonia? Well, first of all it's interesting to notice that this is a country that actually behaves rather like a start-up. It thinks on its feet and everybody knows what's going on. It isn't bound by previous conventions, and that makes it super adaptable. It has a peer-to-peer type structure at its core. In other words, Estonia the country, is actually behaving rather like a platform.

If Uber is the world's biggest taxi company and yet owns no vehicles (with the exception of the driverless ones it's developing of course ...) and Airbnb is the world's biggest accommodation provider yet owns no real estate, you could say that Estonia is the first country that has a population that doesn't populate its land.

Estonia is behaving exactly like a platform.

President Ilves said that he didn't understand why only one state can validate the identity of the citizen. He is a very forward-thinking man and has a team around him that has created a soft infrastructure of government that delivers safety and security for its people without excessive hard leadership. In other words, Estonia is a thoroughly modern place to be a citizen. No wonder it has such a vibrant start-up culture and a very technology-oriented young population.

As well as giving the residents of Estonia an e-identity, the Estonian authorities asked themselves why they couldn't compete for interesting virtual inhabitants. After all, they were rapidly designing an e-country, so why not have virtual citizens?

So beside normal civilians, they have also virtual civilians from all over the world. People can have a digital identity and gain e-residence that enables them to do all kinds of official things like starting businesses, getting access to banking services, etc. without physically being in Estonia. The goal is to connect 10 million Estonian e-residents into the community there. They already have a very healthy start-up scene, and this could take them up to a new level of success where they, as a nation, punch way above their weight. We had talked about digitisation already, and this is the ultimate expression of it. You can become a virtual resident of a tiny Baltic country without ever going there, and be welcomed with open arms.

Sadly, most countries in the world aren't starting from a blank slate and not much in the way of legacy institutions to cramp our style. So the question has to be: in light of all the pressures, digitisation, and the changing nature of jobs, how are we going to be governed in the future? And what effect might that have on the businesses that we plan and design today?

Before we can answer those questions, we need to revisit why we have governments in the first place. Before we can see what our governments are going to look like in the future, we need to understand how they came to be what they are today, and why the forces of nature mean that the way we organise our societies is in for a massive shift.

Governments are big. They need to be because we, as a collective group of humans, need to be organised. As the number of individuals grows (that can be cells or people), the problems of stability start to emerge and a central system to allow things to keep going needs to exist. That's why governments came to be there in the first place. Our systems needed some help and some controls in order to work in everyone's interests. Governments regulated our financial systems, set up our emergency services, and designed our education systems.

Security for the Masses

In early history, there were strong leaders that gave us security and a level of stability. They weren't always very democratic, but they did the job that needed to be done. The simple need to get things done, however crudely, is always the case at the beginning of any cycle. Growing structures and increasing numbers of 'units' (whether those units are cells or people) need certain things to survive. They need security, food, energy and the basic necessities of life. This basic Wave 1.0 requirement applies to every living structure, and communities of people are no exception. As groups of people start to get bigger, then the groups need more help to ensure that all parts of the community have what they need to survive. That inevitably means that early leaders don't tend to be terribly sophisticated. They are there to promote survival of the group, and not much else.

So in the early days, big communities need strong leaders who get things done effectively. Looking back through history there are plenty of famed leaders like Genghis Khan, the Egyptian pharaohs and Julius Caesar; they were all good examples of strong leaders who helped the people they ruled get most of their basic needs met. They might not have all been too sophisticated in their approach but the command and control structures they put in place did bring a level of order out of chaos. That order made sure that the majority of basic needs of the majority of the population were met.

This is the beginning of a 1.0 wave. During Wave 1.0, things reach a critical mass; a certain level of maturity and size exists and that creates new problems. A core Wave 1.0 problem is generally a logistics problem of making sure there is enough to go around and being able to move those things around to the parts that need the supplies. There is a clear need for structure and organisation, and any growing group or organism needs some help with logistics.

Just think of your own body. You need physical stability. You need food, shelter, warmth, water, and safety. Traditionally, governments and leaders simply provide this for us all on a larger scale. Early governments were based on hierarchy and power. They imposed rules. It is our human need for safety that gives us the tolerance for others to wield power over us. That's why we tolerate being told what to do. It's a trade-off and we know it, and the powerful know it.

It's a delicate balance of power and tolerance. But for the first time in our history, that balance really is changing at a fundamental level. It's changing because technology is changing everything. We are getting much better at our own logistics; we don't need people to organise things centrally anymore, in the way that we used to. We have technology platforms that allow us to do that for ourselves, and that has profound implications.

Who is going to Rule Us?

In previous years, raw power was the only way to enforce behaviours. For much of the twentieth century, many of our needs were met by the state. That's certainly the case in Europe. For example, in my home country of the Netherlands, all the critical elements of society were taken care of by the state. Postal services, TV, telecom services, our power systems, healthcare, water and sewage; they were all state-run in the twentieth century. With that much done for us, it's hardly surprising that we put up with all the rules and regulations and law enforcement. After all, we like to play fair and we understand that we need some boundaries if that's going to happen. So we put up with it because all those systems are the basis for growth and development.

Also, having a government allows us to centralise things and develop complex and expensive solutions and spread the costs across the population. Even as far back as the Romans, the population knew that the senate looked after them by controlling much of what was needed for daily life: water systems, planning, waste water, food, agriculture, and trading regulations. So the population had its needs met, and tolerated the taxation that paid for it and the registration of people in exchange for the stability provided.

It makes sense why the Romans were so successful. But like all things, there is a limit to exponential growth. Massive growth leads to greater and greater control, trying to coordinate the uncontrollable. Things get bloated and inefficient. Things that get too big tend to get sluggish and slow. It happens in the animal kingdom too. There's a limit to scalability, and downsides that come with excessive size. Ask any dinosaur.

Like all things, it's a balancing act because governments actually need to be rigid. In fact, it's actually a requirement of good government. No rigidity equals no solid foundation. Lots of things need a level of rigidity built in for them to work; your skeleton and your house are good examples. In the early days of development, everything needs to have a physical infrastructure. That's because without something that doesn't actually change very much, you can't predict anything. But it can't stay rigid, and it can't keep growing indefinitely. Nothing can.

So the first sign of change is watching to see when the big tasks are distributed to smaller, more specialised operators.

It happens in Nature too. Coral is a good example. It's rigid, it's slow-growing, and it gets enormous. It might not be the fastest organism in the sea but its very rigidity and size allows a whole ecosystem to exist because it is there – just like our lumbering and slow governments allow us to grow and thrive. But they don't stay like that forever, and this time, in our technologically more advanced world, we are going to see a different type of change. Instead of governments being toppled in traditional ways, we are going to see the role of governments undermined by people taking things into their own hands.

A great example is the recent projects by entrepreneurs to start making inroads into global problems previously only tackled by governments or large agencies like NATO or international aid agencies. The Bill and Melinda Gates Foundation has made it a mission to eradicate some diseases and take on massive projects in the education and healthcare sectors. Mark Zuckerberg (founder of Facebook) and his wife Priscilla Chan recently pledged $3 billion to fight disease. In previous generations, these sorts of projects were the preserve of governments; now they are increasingly becoming the territory of successful entrepreneurs.

The Future is Virtual Government

Nature demands local expertise, and that's also what you see in our culture. We are seeing more and more trends where people are looking for local solutions inside our local communities so that we don't depend on our governments, reducing reliance on big structures (like the European Union, banks, and large corporations).

We are increasingly trying to solve most of the problems in a local way. It's not always easy, because there are always political arguments about economies of scale and centralised efficiency. But Nature doesn't work that way, and increasingly we are trying to keep things local. Thankfully, because we are increasingly empowered by technology it's getting easier to do.

Nature curbs excesses from within. In communities, you see that when there are people who are disturbing the system, the community catches up with them and throws them out of the community. That's now happening in virtual communities too. Facebook's platform is allowing members of communities to do everything, from finding lost pets to catching criminals. If someone says something outrageous on social media, they are thrust out of the group. The combined power of communities and communication systems is starting to create the ability for us to self-govern.

basic survival needs by themselves. Technology has helped to develop solutions to our basic survival challenges so effectively that most of our Wave 1.0 basic human needs are now fulfilled by smart technology that is still becoming exponentially better and cheaper.

In 2030 it's highly likely that almost all of us are now able to generate and store our own energy, grow our own ecological food in urban and home micro-farms; we will be able to monitor our own health with smart sensors, cloud-based artificial intelligence, and 3D-printed medication from the comfort of our own homes. Advanced new materials and 3D printers enable us to build our products and homes faster and extremely efficiently.

So What's Even Left for Our Governments To Do in 2030?

Well, it's now a case of structuring, monitoring, and enforcing an open-source law system and making sure that the laws are applied fairly. In the same way that the highly successful open-source operating system Linux was created by an open-source community, now laws are also being created by the community. When you think about it, our laws are just like an operating system. An operating system that's created by people working in harmony with each other, and for the good of the many, has a good chance of running a community efficiently and fairly. It's a law of Nature, as you know. A 2030 open-source law development process is likely to be an entirely open and transparent process where the government only has a curating role. Think of a community that works more like Wikipedia – and that means a future without so many lawyers having to interpret things for us. Now, that's a future worth fighting for!

As with all community projects (even one as serious as the maintenance of the rules and boundaries of laws that govern the behaviour of individuals), there always needs to be a curator and an arbitrator. Our government of 2030 will probably curate the process and guide it, but the actual content of the law is likely to be created and maintained by the community itself. That leaves governments to do what governments should do: serve and empower the community, not enforce its will on it and rule it. This is the only way our laws are going to be able to adapt and change fast enough and stay relevant for our fast-changing technology and populations. In 2030 our laws will be more universal, like the DNA information in our cells; there will be multiple versions of the truth at the same time at multiple places, and they will be synchronised real-time all the time.

So how will we prevent fraud? Well, I believe that the law will be distributed automatically using some kind of blockchain principle. Laws that are more generic are likely to be shared over the world with other communities, forming a more general or universal law. When changes are made and accepted, wiki-style, the law will be updated on all the other locations of the truth, so everybody can monitor what is happening and see how the law evolves and adapts to its fast-changing environment. Government functions will largely exist out of multiple smaller online communities with people who know about, care about, and have the ability to influence a certain political topic. The smart community software that structures these political communities automatically incorporates the laws as they are created. It's likely that our technology will be so fast and so interconnected that all the agreements that are made within these communities will automatically conform to the latest version of the law.[7]

The Big Ethics Question

Another important role of government is to set and hold a moral and ethical role in our society. Technology evolves so fast and impacts our society so deeply that as we get more and more connected and everything happens at a faster pace, there will be more ethical questions to answer. How do we set standards and ethics around the use of new technology and how do we apply those rules for the greatest good and the fairest outcome? Governments may still have this moral and ethical role in our societies of the future. Time will tell.

There are some interesting new developments happening right now in this area. Using a combination of peer-to-peer communication platforms, blockchain technology, and an increasingly decentralised World Wide Web platform called Ethereum allows you to take back control over your own online identity without allowing people to cause harm. It's clever technology that has the potential to build up your online 'reputation' on the blockchain by securely and privately, documenting your behaviour through code, without depending on a centralised identity provider organisation or government. This is what the co-founder of the Ethereum platform, Joseph Lubin, has to say:

---

[7] https://futurism.com/you-can-start-your-own-country-thanks-to-web-3-0/

Persistent, portable blockchain-based reputation will enfranchise you as a global citizen. Through reputation, you gain the power to exchange value, get a micro-loan from halfway across the world to start your business (even if you're a refugee without a bank account), to execute contracts with other trusted parties that you'll never need to meet. You can do this free from the inefficiencies of an esoteric, centralised system you need the help of lawyers, government agents, and other intermediaries to understand and navigate.

Lubin goes on to say:

This future may sound like science fiction, but to those of us who work with blockchain and Ethereum, as decentralised tools become more readily available to us every day, it is fast turning into our reality. In time we can all be presidents of certain communities we care about.

Lubin is also the founder of the cleverly named ConsenSys, a company on a mission to 'create simplified and automated decentralised applications (dApps) to facilitate peer-to-peer transactions and exchanges'.

Systems like ConsenSys and the increasingly wide use of blockchain technology start to give us a glimpse forward in time and help us start to grasp the magnitude and speed of change. It's becoming clear that technology and the imaginative minds behind many of these new ideas are going to supersede many aspects of government, and it's not going to take very long for that to happen.

No wonder so many politicians are scared. They know change is coming, but they don't realise just how fast it's happening.

But you do. You have an incredible opportunity to use your knowledge and foresight wisely.

How Will We Spend Our Free Time in 2030?

By the time we get to the mature phase of a Wave 1.0 (which we will do by 2030 if Nature's laws, and the exponential growth of technology that mirrors it, suggests we will), our basic income will probably be fully taken care of.

If that sounds expensive don't worry, because our basic income requirements are likely to be much smaller than they are now. Does that sound far-fetched? On the surface, yes, but when you think about it more deeply, probably not. That's because when your energy and food needs are taken care of from home with cheap technology, and you print and recycle most things you need without having to travel, then basic income needs shrink to a fraction of what they are now. By 2030 it's quite possible that basic income is now widely accepted, and most countries have incorporated this principle for many of their civilians.

The idea of a universal basic income (UBI) is hitting the headlines more and more. A small-scale trial starts soon in Finland. The trial is set to run over two years and will involve more than 2,000 people. It's only a small sample but it's a significant policy experiment. There's another trial starting soon in a region of the Netherlands, and discussions and debate taking place in Switzerland and even Oakland, California. It's a topic that won't seem to go away; and the political classes haven't quite worked out how to handle it yet.[8]

In an interview towards the end of his US presidency, Barack Obama discussed the massive changes coming. In an interview[9] with *Wired* editor-in-chief, Scott Dadich, and MIT Media Lab director, Joi Ito, the subject featured, and it was interesting that it was even brought up during such difficult times. Although he was careful to stay neutral on the key topic, Obama had clearly grasped the size of the problem on the horizon and commented, 'Whether a universal income is the right model – is it gonna be accepted by a broad base of people? – that's a debate that we'll be having over the next ten or twenty years.'

There have been mentions from commentators on the issue about things like negative income tax so there are no disincentives for being productive. Now, that's an idea that you won't be hearing too many politicians talk about for a while!

So, from the luxury of a hindsight time capsule, we would likely be having a conversation with friends about how, after the introduction of basic income, the economic output of people exploded. When people don't have to worry about their primary needs like food and shelter we can start to focus on our higher needs and purpose, and beautiful things start to happen! Creativity and living for a higher purpose won't just be something the rich can indulge in – it will be something that everyone whose basic needs have been met will be able to do.

---

[8] https://futurism.com/thousands-to-receive-basic-income-in-finland/
[9] https://www.wired.com/2016/10/president-obama-mit-joi-ito-interview/

In 2030, since the introduction of the basic income, areas like culture, sport, and recreation have exploded. People can now enjoy life to the full. When virtual reality and mixed reality technology became mature, a complete new cultural, sports, and recreational infrastructure formed (it's already started – Candy Crush, anyone?). People are now able to join all kind of events all over the world without travelling. And by using photorealistic virtual/mixed reality devices, it feels like actually being there with all your senses. The line between actually being there physically or virtually is very hard to detect. We are already heading towards hologram calls; the future isn't as far away as you might think ...

Beam Me Up, Scotty

I know some of the things I talk about might seem a little far-fetched, yet the same could be said for some of the science fiction creations from the early days of programmes like *Star Trek*. Yet those very 'fictional' items are now everyday items in all our pockets. Think about mobile communication devices (iPhone), instant food (3D-printed food), the translation devices (voice translator phone apps) and some of the medical treatments (needleless injections), and many more, which were all illustrated as fantasy back in the early TV series. Many of the things we take for granted today seemed far-fetched back in the early days of *Star Trek* but are everyday objects today. So let's get back to what people will be doing and how it changes the nature of how we are governed.

What Nature Teaches Us

If you have the belief that 'people don't do things for nothing', then just look around you at how much gets done for a non-commercial return already. When I'm out working with organisations, people I meet are often sceptical about the idea of people doing what they love for a minimal commercial return, and yet there is plenty of evidence that shows many of us do that already. There are a lot of people who do what they love to do, for no financial return at all. Ask people working on charitable projects, organising sports for local children, visiting sick or elderly people in their homes for no wage – things they do because they want to contribute. As well as service, we all do things for free all the time. Everywhere around you, people are doing what they are born to do, from coding open-source software for free, to adding to the sum of human knowledge on Wikipedia for free, to climbing mountains because they are there, and doing valuable community work for no visible, tangible return at all. It happens because we don't live in a world of mere tangibles. Nature shows us that this is part of life. We all do things because we are compelled to do things, not just because we are rewarded. Allow me to elaborate.

Consider this. Lung cells don't get paid to extract oxygen from the air. Heart cells don't get paid to beat. Just like the cells in our body do things they evolved to do, people all over our planet are ready to do the things they were born to do. There just hasn't always been an elegant or efficient way of rewarding them fully.

In the future I believe we will be able to trade value in more sophisticated ways than we have up until now. It's going to get easier and easier to do what we were born to do and in return get food and warmth from the community we live in.

Humans in a society will be able to be a more valued part of a coherent community in the same natural way that cells from our own bodies play a vital role doing what they were created to do – without being directly paid. All that happens in our bodies; cells' intrinsic needs are taken care of by the community they are all a part of. Nature went there first, and we now have an opportunity to learn and model the patterns. It's a challenge how we can do the same and live and look after our fellow humans in the way that nature intended.

What Our Cells can Teach us about Our 1.0 Future

The cells in our body have the ability to generate energy, store energy, and they are highly efficient because they only use the energy they really need. Cells are able to repair themselves and in that process they recycle almost everything within the cell itself. In other words, biology is sustainable, renewable, and virtually self-sufficient.

Technology is consistently mimicking the miracle that's taking place in our cells. I believe we are likely to see more local, sustainable, self-organising solutions where we will all become less dependent on current government structures. We will increasingly live in self-sufficient communities, independent from physical government. Add those elements together and it's obvious that because we will all be more independent, there will be no need for many of the controls that exist today. Local rules and regulations will be more local, and will be constantly adapting to the needs of the community. Communities will be based more and more on

It's not just groups of neighbours, or people with common interests though. Companies and platforms are doing it too. For example, with Uber, the taxi driver rates the client and the client rates the taxi driver. If there is a bad taxi driver then people say, 'I don't want to be picked up by that guy again.' In time, the whole community starts to steer clear and the bad driver doesn't get any work, so the system works for the greater good of the user community. Bad passengers get the same treatment, and so the community of taxi drivers get to avoid the people who make life difficult. TripAdvisor was an early example of helping consumers avoid places where the marketing hype didn't match the experience. It transformed the travel industry, and – even a few short years later – we now take being able to do travel research for granted. It's the first time in history we have been able to do that, and it's opened up the world for many people to travel safely. A global society of travellers has created a database of experience that we can all benefit from.

What Will Governments Be Doing in 2030?

So what are our governments around the world going to look like by 2030, knowing that Moore's law and Rose's law will have transformed the nature of our technology?

I believe most governments will be either lightweight digital or virtual. They will be highly connected with the civilian population, to the point that the government and the society it services will be more like a single entity. It will become more of a self-correcting system that keeps it's own balance (just like everything in Nature does eventually) and we will see an explosion of real-time and direct democracy.

If I was writing this in 2030, I would probably be telling you that the traditional government structures from the beginning of the century were just too slow to keep up with the exponential change and fast-growing needs of our information-driven communities. More and more government processes were outsourced to organisations and smart communities. As a result, the role of governments had to evolved really quickly and because people could give feedback in real time, the old-fashioned institutions had rapidly become less dominant and evolved to a more virtual institution. The number of people that work in the government has shrunk dramatically, and the people that are still working for the government only monitor the automated processes.

In the last decade more and more people have become able to fulfil their interests and shared values; this is happening already and you can read more about what's happening in the trends section. Even our food is going to be grown hyper locally (even in our own homes) and energy will be localised too. We look at energy in more detail in Wave 2.0 though that changing technology is going to have a dramatic impact on our societies and the way we interact with each other.

Society is going to change faster in the next twenty years than we have probably seen in the last three generations. How we interact is going to change in ways many people just can't imagine right now. It's going to change how we do business, how we communicate, how we are governed, and how we interact socially. Are you ready for the big social wave?

There are many developments that haven't reached the mainstream media yet, so I've gathered some of the most interesting, fun, and transformational ones together for you. Seeing the trends and some of the early-stage technology out there being tested will give you an early indication of trends that are about to go mainstream. If you are in business, you are going to need it!

Chapter 20
Wave 1.0 – Trends

A Hyper Local Future

I believe that over time, more things will be solved locally. Brexit may be an early example of the start of this trend. Big governments are slow and they can't change as quickly as the communities they serve. I think that our collective groups of people with a common interest will take more and more care of our basic needs, and our governments are going to be left with less and less to do. Of course, we will always need some form of organisation; we will always probably need some centralised organisations that control some elements of our society – things like law enforcement, justice and certain elements of healthcare like the care of the vulnerable people in our communities. We are always going to need people to organise things and take care of people.

Things are already heading in this direction in many countries. For example, in the UK, government policy has been towards 'care in the community' for some time. In the Netherlands it's even become a planning policy requirement to build a granny flat for housing elderly parents when you build a new house. Our policymakers know that the government won't be able to look after all our elderly; we are living in a demographic time bomb. Thankfully, technology can and will help.

Care on the Doorstep

We have all seen examples of institutions that have treated people in less-than-humane ways. Technology is going to enable us to move towards a hyper local society once again. It will be practical to be hyper local when we can all have what we need without having to travel and when we can generate our own energy at home.

The process of Humanification can take place when the cycle of big government starts to dissolve and is replaced with smaller units of people who live and thrive with the facilities that are on our own doorstep. It's often referred to by some political commentators as creeping privatisation, but actually it's simply a natural progression. For example, in many countries healthcare has already been partially consumerised because it's just too big for any one organisation to handle.

Governments will need to transfer responsibility to families, private companies, and local communities in order to cope with increasing demand. We will go from huge units to smaller ones.

The 'Grow Your Own' Trend

I believe it's highly likely that we are going to grow more and more food ourselves at home. The developments going on in both biotech and energy mean that the increased reprogramming of the DNA of plants is going to allow us to grow things in conditions that could not be reproduced on a large scale.

Currently, there is still a great deal of fear around DNA plant programming, but I think in the future we will know more and more about what makes a good vegetable and what it will take to grow one that contains enough healthy nutrients. I think we are still in the early phases of this research; it's definitely only a Wave 1.0 technology at the moment. There is still a considerable amount of R&D required before we see the new fruits of this wave in our own fridges.

Agritech moving away from the fields of farmers to our homes and gardens is an important thing to watch out for. I believe that eventually we will be able to grow our entire meal at home and that we will be growing more in urban environments and growing at an industrial scale away from traditional agricultural environments too. There are already many examples of pioneering vertical and robotic farms that are starting to go mainstream. These new-style 'farms' involve a tiny amount of soil and water, and they are able to create a huge amount of food. The early days of hydroponic farming did change the way we grew food as far back as the 1970s, but then the technology languished for a while. There has been a resurgence of interest in how to move things further and taking a fresh look at farming has started to gain traction again.

Up until now, if you wanted to farm products such as vegetables, you have to be skilled as a farmer. But robotic farms have started to change that concept completely.

A Japanese company, Spread, is moving to full robotic production and will be producing 50,000 lettuces per day without any human intervention. The only human hand involved is the one that plants the seeds. After that, the entire production process, including re-planting young seedlings to watering, trimming, and harvesting crops, will be done by the robots. With LED lighting, energy costs have been slashed, and 98% of the water used is recycled. It's transforming production and minimising land use.

In the future I believe you will be able to grow any kind of vegetable you fancy yourself. I can visualise being able to download a specific software program to grow a specific type of vegetable. In my view, it won't be long before everybody will be able to grow vegetables without any knowledge about farming. That's going to be a big shift, and it has incredible potential. Technological developments like this are going to allow us to reimagine some clever ways of using some of the spaces we already have, including things like the rooftops of our existing buildings.

I foresee a time in the near future when you will be able to buy a machine for your house that grows your vegetables at a rapid pace. It will probably look like your fridge, but will instead create the perfect microclimate and conditions needed to provide you with all the healthy organic food you need to feed your family. Imagine that.

The Good vs Profits Trend

Another big trend we are going to see is increasingly moving towards doing things for the right reasons. Put simply, I believe we are going to get less selfish.

Commercial companies are extrinsically motivated; they build something or deliver something to make more profit for the shareholders. A community is there because it is intrinsically motivated for the survival of the whole community. So after Wave 1.0 survival needs are taken care of, we are, as humans, compelled to create something useful or beautiful.

That whole process, and where we end up because of it, will be driven by the empowerment of the individual. That is the process of Humanification and it's all enabled by our technology, computing power, and our imagination. It will give us power that connects and brings us together. It will give us power that will allow us to function more as a single organism, and the power to become a giant collective of humanity that's working as one.

The Age of True Eco-cycling

In many western countries, we are already recycling and reusing more and more old materials. Thankfully, the conscience of the western world is finally starting to go mainstream and most consumers and many of our institutions are finally starting to recognise the common sense of not becoming ever more disposable in our way of living. It's almost become a lifestyle statement.

The term 'Eco-cycling' was coined some time ago now and it's become a part of our language in most western countries. While most people use the language without considering what it really means, industry insiders and innovators have been working hard to find ways to repurpose waste materials. Now there is the technology to turn plastics into concrete-compatible new building materials. We are turning recycled plastic bottles into railway sleepers. There is a device (development funded by Coca-Cola) that turns waste Coke bottles into a 3D-printing filament, equivalent to 3D printer 'ink'. It's a cradle-to-cradle solution, with no harmful chemicals. Just like things get recycled in nature, Coke's most popular product container is now reusing itself.

Re-Inventing Medicine

There are astonishing developments in the biotech area. Maybe you have heard of CRISPR, the gene-editing technology?

CRISPR has had massive funding as it seems to offer an effective way to edit the genes of any species – including humans. Previously, gene editing methods have taken months (or even years), while CRISPR speeds that time up to mere weeks. CRISPR offers the potential to cut and splice genes so quickly and so precisely it has potential applications for creating new biofuels, materials, drugs, and foods within much shorter time frames at a relatively low cost.

Researchers essentially trick bacteria into cutting strands of DNA at a precise spot, where they can then replace, change, or disable a gene. In the most exciting scenario, CRISPR would make it possible to treat genetic diseases such as sickle cell anaemia and muscular dystrophy.

It's a great example of the rise of nanotechnology – that's where we start to intervene or create things on a molecular level. We are already starting to see the rise of very small robots, motors, engines, or bots that are becoming so small they can be injected.

All this new materials technology will enable us to create more and more new materials and applications for them. We will have new ways to create computer chips, change the face of our solar technology (more on that later), develop applications for the previously hailed 'miracle' material graphene – a single-atom layer of hyper-conductive carbon with extraordinary qualities. Graphene is material that has amazing potential. There is already work going on that uses graphene to extract electricity and water from air. Imagine what this could mean for underdeveloped countries!

If we can generate energy and water from graphene, then many of the world's problems could be solved in one stroke. Perhaps it won't be long before you have some kind of graphene resource extraction device in your home that pulls air through some membranes and gives you clear water and some electricity that's almost for free. Now, I'm fully aware that our political and power systems will have to undergo massive changes to cope with this, and that in some ways it's not going to be easy; but change will come.

I'm an optimist and think that the largest majority of us want peace and prosperity for our fellow man. By giving people the power of their own lives, in time, better choices will be made and the old power-based economies and leaders will either adapt or wither and die.

Chapter 21

Summer 2030 –
How Will we be Living?

August 10th, 2030

It is 2030 and many governments have already transformed into digital or virtual governments. The traditional government structures were much too slow to keep up with the exponential change and fast-growing needs of the community.

People are now able to fulfil most of their basic human needs by themselves, by using technology that is becoming exponentially better and cheaper. People are able to generate and store their own energy and grow their own food.

How will our healthcare systems change? Back in the twentieth century, doctors focused on symptoms. In 2030 we now look at causes. We are now the CEO of our own health. We have direct feedback from smart devices. Our Apple watches tell us to move around when we have been sedentary for too long. Our watches will also remind us to breathe in a more relaxed way.

There is less for governments to do because now we grow most of our own food, we stay more healthy, and reduce the need for health services. Now small things can be detected by technology, and most of our first line healthcare is virtualised.

Even in the early twenty-first century, IBM's Watson computer was giving 90% accuracy on cancer diagnosis. It was able to read up to 200 million documents, research papers and journals in the blink of an eye, compared to real doctors who took weeks to form a diagnosis using invasive, lengthy, and expensive tests. We are in an age of e-health. Today, our home medical dispensers print 3D pills! You can scan your own DNA and print your own personal medicines. There's a new kind of robot, and 'he/she/it' dispenses your medicine for you and all the other people in town or village. The robot 'talks' to your doctor to make sure you take your medicine. All that reduces the need for quite so much nursing. All in all, despite our ageing populations, computing power, artificial intelligence, and robotics are all going to help to reduce the strains on our global medical system. And we are going to need it.

Chapter 22

Wave 2.0 – What is the Future for our Infrastructure?

How Nature Solves the Stability Problem

Stability. In some way, we all seek it. We seek it in our relationships, we seek it in our careers, in our businesses, and from our communities. Yet we don't live in a stable world. We are all part of a living system that changes in some way every single moment. Everything in our universe, including us, is in a permanent state of flux, growth, development, or moving towards being 'recycled'. Yet all organisms crave stability. We crave it, probably more than most. At the very least, we are consciously aware of our own need for it.

The existence of Wave 2.0 is the solution to the stability challenge that was encountered as Wave 1.0 built up. As things multiply, they get more and more unstable as the system gets bigger.

What happened during Wave 1.0 created the need and set the foundation. Wave 2.0 is simply the phase of growth where there is some sort of infrastructure built. That's the infrastructure that a) holds things together and b) connects the various parts with all the systems and functions the thing needs to survive.

So how do you predict when it's time to move from a Wave 1.0 to a Wave 2.0?

To predict the formation of a Wave 2.0 you need to first understand what this wave looks like, why it came to be, and what powers it. There is a 2.0 wave going on somewhere at this very moment. That's a business opportunity for someone, an innovation strategy for someone, and a significant shift for a person, a country, or a place. So would you agree it would be rather useful to be able to spot the Wave 2.0 signs?

First of all, it's useful to know that all Wave 2.0s are all driven by the same engine, whether that be in nature, in technology or in our own development. The formation is always driven by a need that must be met.

So let's look at our human needs first because it's easy to connect the dots with ourselves (as human beings) at the centre of the picture.

Think back to the hierarchy of human needs we spoke about earlier – Maslow's pyramid. At the bottom of the pyramid is the first level that underpins the whole structure of our being: our need for physical safety. Without that, we don't exist! Without physical safety and security, our ancestors would have been at the bottom of a swamp somewhere, or in the belly of a sabre-toothed tiger – and you wouldn't be reading this. So in Wave 1.0 we adopted survival strategies that allowed us to live long enough to want more from life. So we move up to the second level of the pyramid. This is our equivalent of Wave 2.0 needs.

Here, in this second level, lies the need all living things have for a level of security. This is a need beyond having the water, shelter, and nutrition to keep us alive and reproduce; it moves into having the knowledge that we can meet our needs in the future. The security to know we can sleep at night without being attacked by barbarians and live in relative comfort and a place of stability.

All living things need this; we humans need it, plants need it, animals need it, and so do our cells. We need some security beyond mere survival.

But here's where things get more complicated. Stability is, by nature, not a fixed quality. It's stability, not rigidity. There's nothing strong about something that's not adapting to its environment. The stability that Maslow was talking about is more about a need for a viable balance between extremes. A balance and stability that allows us to find some regularity somewhere in the middle; a place where survival is more predictable and tolerable than it was inside Wave 1.0.

But we are not as unique in this as we might think we are. All groups of living cells have the same need. Biologists refer to this stability as homeostasis. Bear with me, because, despite its fancy name, the concept itself is quite simple and highly relevant to being able to recognise a Wave 2.0.

Nature's Big Balancing Act

Homeostasis is simply an absence of major destabilising forces. The Wikipedia definition is:

[T]he property of a system in which a variable (for example, the concentration of a substance in solution, or its temperature) is actively regulated to remain very nearly constant.

Any system that's growing has a natural struggle with this maintaining a balance between growing and maintaining stability. A plant that grows too fast above ground struggles to have roots deep enough to pull the water in. A plant that grows well below ground but doesn't have enough leaf can't get the chlorophyll it needs to survive. There's always a balance. Do you grow leaves, or do you grow roots? Nature is good at making those decisions. Traditionally, groups of humans aren't so good at it; at least, they haven't been that good at doing it in a sustainable way.

It's All About the Infrastructure

So it's during the Wave 2.0 phase that the need for an infrastructure that can cope with demand turns out to be the major challenge. Until that's solved, nothing can move forward any further.

The MRI scans of our own neural networks look remarkably similar to the patterns of our physical communications networks, like our telecoms systems and the internet. Nature gave us the pattern and we almost subconsciously followed it, and for good reason.

That's no accident, but nor was it quite deliberate design. It just so happens that communities of cells and communities of humans have the same problems to solve and the same solutions to solve them. It's inevitable that we came up with similar patterns to solve the problems.

Growth and control of infrastructure is one of history's triggers for some of the most epic battles, empires gained and lost, and it was how the West was won. Vast fortunes are made and lost over infrastructure. Kingdoms and power bases have been overthrown over an infrastructure. The control of rivers, roads, mountain passes, oil pipelines, railways – the list goes on and on. Building of infrastructure allows survival; control over it dictates who is in charge!

Throughout history there seems to have been a ceiling or a maximum size that any community can get to before it starts to crumble. In recent history, we have seen the breakdown of the USSR and the challenges facing the European Union. The challenge of finding balance isn't easy because it's hard to force different cultures to live and work together.

One big global community has not been possible in the past because there wasn't a shared global infrastructure, there were no global telecom capabilities, no global automation capabilities, minimal global sharing capabilities, no globally available learning capabilities, and – until recently – precious little in the way of global co-creation capabilities.

When you look at what nature teaches us, it's hardly surprising that the challenges of a big organism, system, or population can be overcome. There is a light at the end of the tunnel. Nature always succeeds in finding a balance, and I believe we can too, and our ability to harness technology is THE defining factor.

So How Does Wave 2.0 Work?

But before we dive into what the future might hold for our infrastructure, it will only be useful for you if you have some increased processing power of your own. By that, I mean that you gain a new level of understanding about the way Wave 2.0 works so you have the ability to spot the wave building in situations around you.

But before we can predict the future, we need to grasp some key lessons from the past, because it's in Wave 2.0 where useful infrastructures, that propel things forward, start to be built, and there are plenty of examples that demonstrate it perfectly.

The Tale of An American Merchant

In 1880 the Smith family had had enough. They were American merchants who were moving on from their home and business that had, up until that day, been located in the state of Georgia in the USA. Today, they were on the move. Mr Smith had achieved a level of success with the family business, but they just couldn't expand. Any growth in Mr Smith's business had been blighted by the limitations of moving their goods around. That's why he had decided to move the family. To get to the next stage they needed better hard infrastructure. They needed reliable transportation for themselves and their goods. They needed to get away from roads that were muddy in the winter and dusty in the summer. When the Smiths tried to move heavy cargo on the roads with horses and wagons, the weather, the ground conditions, and the inevitable lame horses always seemed to get in the way. There was always the river, but that was treacherous at times. It worked well when goods needed to be moved downstream, but when they were trying to move goods upstream, it was time-consuming, expensive, and unreliable.

When the railroad came to Georgia everything changed, and the Smiths needed to get close to it.

Georgia had moved into Wave 2.0. The age of infrastructure had reached the Deep South. Not only did everything change in the next few years for families like the Smiths, but the big capitalist barons of the nineteenth and twentieth centuries made the fortunes of their generation.

This was the age of the Vanderbilt, Rockefeller and Carnegie. The infrastructure that these industrialists provided went on to solve many of the stability problems caused by an expanding population – people like the Smiths, who previously couldn't thrive because they couldn't get around efficiently. When the railroads, oil pipelines, and shipping connected people together it lifted America to become one of the most prosperous nations on earth. That would allow for the system to start to flourish and new disruptive technologies to emerge. For the Smiths, all they had to do was go with the flow.

The Big Smoke

We are now at the turn of the twenty-first century and after 200 years of coal- and oil-based infrastructure, we live in a highly polluted world and our ecosystem is at dangerous tipping point. So, how did that happen? And, more to the point, why did it happen?

When you understand how and why a Wave 2.0 forms, it all starts to make sense.

You saw what happened in Georgia to the Smith family. They were part of a fast-growing community that their business served. It brought a massive potential upside for a thriving family business, but it also brought challenges with it that forced change, disruption, and – eventually – innovation. That's a Wave 2.0 in action. When a community starts to grow exponentially fast, more and more needs have to be fulfilled. In a human Wave 2.0 like the one in the early twentieth century, we need more construction materials, more logistic solutions, more money, more energy, more of everything in fact.

As is often the case, governments (the 'soft' infrastructures that are institutions rather than physical 'hard' infrastructures like roads) can't fulfil all the need quickly enough. This fuels a fast-growing gap between what governments provide and what people need for their families and communities to thrive.

Back in the days of the industrial pioneers in the US, you see that commercial entities saw an opportunity to bridge the ever-expanding gap. Industry and mass production was the answer, and the Industrial Revolution was born. Incidentally, the same Wave 2.0 process had occurred in Victorian England too and played out following almost exactly the same pattern.

The first primary need that gets filled has to be logistics. Just like the body needs a logistics system to help oxygen, water, and nutrients to reach the outer edges of your body, a country needs to move things around efficiently so that the cells (people!) can thrive. In the USA, the logistics systems that changed everything got started with fleets of steamboats that transported people and goods, but soon boats were outdated and too slow. Vanderbilt build the largest shipping empire in the world, built the entire infrastructure on water to ship people and goods from A to B through the entire country. At the peak of his empire, Cornelius Vanderbilt sold his entire fleet and invested in railroads instead (transcontinental railroads). Vanderbilt bought railroad company after railroad company and he became the biggest railroad magnate in America.

So what effect did this have on the wider system? Well, laying rail tracks was a high-performance engine for unprecedented growth because it provided 180,000 jobs, allowing the economy to explode, even before the railroads were finished. Transcontinental built hubs to connect multiple railroads tracks (including Grand Central Depot in New York), and situated on twenty-two acres it was to become the biggest building in New York at the time.

When Vanderbilt teamed up with John D. Rockefeller, he made an exclusive deal to transport oil over his railroads and what was explosive growth went exponential. Rockefeller, another legendary industrialist, was now able to bring energy (his Standard Oil) to every house in the nation.

The story doesn't stop there because soon Rockefeller wanted to be independent from the railroads. He needed his own infrastructure. Instead, Standard Oil's pipeline replaced the railroads as the way to transport energy from A to B. The exponential wave got the fuel it needed to keep growing. Now heavy industries were able to grow even faster, and the steel industry was born. This allowed Andrew Carnegie's steel business to transport steel over the existing railroads and that, in turn, enabled them to build more and bigger industrial facilities. It contributed directly to people's abilities to grow towns and cities. Mass production of construction steel, railroads, bridges, and buildings was possible because of Andrew Carnegie's steel and it proved to be very profitable for Carnegie indeed.

You can see how having fast and reliable infrastructure became the foundation of a strong country. At the turn of the twentieth century, America was the most rapid-growing country in the world. It had all the right conditions for Wave 2.0, and the rapid response of a group of fast-moving entities allowed it to build with exponential speed and change the history of the world. That is much the situation we are in now with the same exponential growth that's happening right now in the technology field.

But there is a dark side, a price to pay. There always is.

Firstly, there was massive economic disruption. Genuine innovation generally is a result of disruption, or is the cause of it. It wasn't just the infrastructure that was responsible for the productivity explosion. One of the results of Standard Oil fuelling the nation was that people were able to work longer hours because they had light on command. That was a massive disruption in its own right. But the really big disruptions happened during the transitions. With oil now being shipped through pipelines instead of by rail, one-third of America's 360 rail companies went bankrupt, often leaving the owners of the stock penniless. The stock market crashed and the entire economy was on its knees, yet the wealth of the people who owned the infrastructure (and who had the common sense to diversify) still held massive power. Where there is innovation there is disruption.

The other big price is one that we are all still paying today. We are paying the price with the health of our planet. Carbon dioxide has been on an S-curve too. The amount of harmful chemicals we are pumping into the atmosphere is unsustainable. We need disruption and innovation on a massive scale. Luckily, we may just have it.

There is hope. The visionary entrepreneur, Elon Musk, pointed out on the day he launched the Tesla Powerwall, a revolutionary new battery technology for home use: 'We have this handy fusion reactor in the sky called the sun. You don't have to do anything; it just works. It shows up every day and produces ridiculous amounts of power.'

More on Powerwall later. What's important to see is that solar technology is becoming dramatically more efficient, and the price point has dropped dramatically in the past few years and will continue to fall as solar moves into the mainstream. The evolution from Tesla and others in the field of power storage gives us hope that soon we will be able to mimic nature and become self-sustaining and be able to stop using fossil fuels. The latest innovation from Musk was his announcement of camouflaged solar panels that are, in effect, textured glass and quartz tiles with integrated solar cells. The tiles are nearly indistinguishable from conventional tiling. The new roof material and technology are part of Musk's master plan to transform our world into one powered by sustainable energy. You will be reading more about the exciting new developments in power generation, energy storage, and water infrastructure in the trends report at the end of this section.

Our Electric Future

Thanks to Elon Musk, most of us have heard the name Tesla by now. But it's worth noting that the electric revolution started a long time ago, and even the Tesla brand name, which now signifies a revolutionary innovative company, takes its name from a brilliant, innovative scientist and businessman from 100 years ago. All things present have their roots in the past, and that's why it's so important that you know how the roots grew into what we have today.

I'm sure you have heard the name Thomas Edison, who is famous for having invented the lightbulb. What's less well known is the story of one of his apprentices, Nicolas Tesla.

What went on after the lightbulb invention was a tale of a clashing of commercial titans and a vicious rivalry that was to change the face of power distribution, not just for America, but for the whole world.

The most famous banker of the day, J. P. Morgan, saw the potential of electric light. Something that could light every house in the US was clearly a massive opportunity. He not only invested in Thomas Edison; he also hired him to install electric light bulbs in his house. J. P. Morgan's home was the first private home entirely lit by electricity. Although most of us take electricity for granted now, at the time an invisible energy that was safer, easier to distribute, and cheaper than coal or oil was seen as a miracle. Electricity became a must-have for the elite. Electricity became a huge success, so Edison created a central power station to power the entire island of Manhattan, a power station that ran on DC current.

But he had competition. Nicolas Tesla invented AC generators. His ideas weren't going down a storm, so Nicolas Tesla quit his job and founded his own company. This new AC current technology became even more successful than the DC power of Thomas Edison. More and more generators where installed, powering more and more homes in the US. There was a turning point when the Niagara Falls power station needed to choose between AC and DC – it was to set the tone for what would become the future standard. It was an epic battle that even saw Edison trying to convince people that AC was dangerous by electrocuting large animals in public! But it wasn't just the technology that was competing; it was two investors.

Edison had J. P. Morgan on his side, but Nicolas Tesla had the backing of investor George Westinghouse. It was a war of titans. Neither investor was used to being beaten. J. P. Morgan had invested heavily in DC power, and understandably he wanted DC to be the standard. His response? It was classic Wall Street bullying tactics of the day: J. P. Morgan tried to bankrupt Westinghouse and win the Niagara Falls power station contract. But there was something getting in the way: the 1893 World's Fair. You see, the team behind the fair, which was due to take place in Chicago, wanted the fair to be powered by electricity. Westinghouse won the Fair contract and on opening night, when the whole world was watching, 200,000 light bulbs lit up the World's Fair. It was all powered Nicolas Tesla and Westinghouse. You can just imagine the fury of J. P. Morgan.

As a result of a great bit of strategic marketing, Tesla and Westinghouse won the contract for the Niagara Falls power station. J. P. Morgan and Edison were defeated, and AC current became the standard for our electric powered world. AC current is now the building platform for all the electrical equipment we use all over the world.

But that wasn't the end of the story. As one of the most powerful financiers of his time, J. P. Morgan was determined to get his own way. He started a sustained attack on Westinghouse, and even forced him to hand over the AC patents. Then, still not satisfied, J. P. Morgan bought extra shares to eliminate Thomas Edison from their company Edison Electric, and General Electric was born. It became one of the biggest companies of the US, promoting AC current technology. It was a move that consolidated the electric industry. Electricity went mainstream.

So, back to the present day. All of our modern technology is, or will be, powered by electricity very soon. Now you know how much of our infrastructure came into being, you have a much better chance at being ready to see the next wave of infrastructure coming, before it hits your world.

We Need Safety and Comfort

Let's go back to Nature for a moment. In the human body the infrastructure for the absorption and distribution of the building materials for our life, and the energy that powers it, is almost entirely automated. Almost all your organs work autonomously; you don't have to think about the digestion of your food, remember to tell your heart to beat, set an alarm to circulate or filter your blood; it all happens unconsciously. You just get up in the morning, and your personal infrastructure (including your skeleton) just does what it was made to do, and you go about your day.

Your unconscious mind takes care of everything. The processes that allow you to be you are all automated to a very high level. It's all pretty efficient and doesn't cost your body that much in terms of energy expenditure. Evolution saw to it that you have a robust and almost fully automated infrastructure. Any organism with an inefficient infrastructure won't survive for long, so its internal infrastructure has to be very efficient and sustainable to survive.

I believe the same will happen with the infrastructure of humanity. At this moment in time the infrastructure that we have created to sustain ourselves is, ironically, far from sustainable or efficient. We currently have a physical infrastructure that produces huge amounts of harmful pollutants and we are depleting our earth of valuable resources.

As we discussed inside the earlier chapter about 'The Age of the Entrepreneur', more and more global challenges are being addressed by the leaders of global businesses. Many of these mega-entrepreneurs are already looking towards space and other planets to feed our resource-hungry human race with the mineral resources we need.

For example, Jeff Bezos, the founder of Amazon, has recently announced his own space project and set out his vision and what we will need to do to survive into the future. Bezos believes that our needs will in part be met from other planets and he intends to be part of that solution.

It is certainly clear that our current infrastructure is so inefficient and harmful to our ecosystem, and even humanity itself, that something must be done.

Thankfully, there are some brilliant minds and very ambitious thinkers who are contributing to entirely rethinking Wave 2.0, our infrastructure for the twenty-first century and beyond.

I believe that in the near future (and it has already started), people will treat infrastructural processes in a more holistic way instead of as isolated systems. The massive hope for the future is already starting to become reality. It's my prediction that we are heading towards a much more sustainable and autonomous infrastructure based on renewable energy. Remember those S-curves from earlier in the book? My view of the data tells me we are about to see an exponential explosion of sustainable energy at a level that has never been seen before, and it could just be happening in the nick of time.

Recently, an article published by researchers in the journal *Nano Letters* revealed that they have devised a new type of highly efficient photocell.

Nathaniel Gabor, assistant professor for physics and astronomy at the University of California, Riverside, led research spurred on by a simple question as to why plants are green. So Gabor and his team decided to take a fresh look at photosynthesis in plants.[10] That question eventually led to a quest to mimic the remarkable ability to efficiently harvest the sun's energy that plants have built in. The miracle of plants isn't just that they harvest energy; it's that they can do it no matter how erratic the sunlight is. As we have seen so many times before, Nature has already solved the problem, so how can we learn and develop technology to tap into what can already be done by plants? Gabor and his team developed a new-generation quantum heat engine photocell with the ability to regulate the conversion of energy without the need for external controls. That's exactly what plants do, and it's been the Holy Grail for solar energy. The ability to harness energy from the massive thermonuclear reactor in the sky that gives off more energy than we will ever need will change everything for us. It will change how we travel, how we eat, and how we are governed. It will also help to preserve our planet and set off some new trends in fields as diverse as medicine, education, and farming.

So what are the big Wave 2.0 trends? Let's find out next. For bang-up-to-date revelations about what's happening in the world of new technology, visit my website, where I curate some of the freshest thinking and innovations by the brightest and the best minds on the planet. Come and say hello at www.humanification.com. Now let's get on and look at some trends.

---

[10] https://futurism.com/light-harvesting-quantum-photocells-herald-a-new-age-in-solar-energy/

Chapter 23

Wave 2.0 – Infrastructure Trends

The good news is that the infrastructure trends that are emerging now are pointing to a more sustainable infrastructure that has the potential to be largely self-managing. I believe that in the next decade computing power and machine learning algorithms will have increased at an exponential rate. You already know the background to that, and understand the fact that my prediction isn't just pulled out of the air. Our technology and app development is simply following the S-curve that has a fairly accurate level of predictive power. As a result, computers will be able to learn things that only we humans are able to do now.

Computers will very soon be driving our cars for us (that's already a reality, we just aren't ready with the soft infrastructure like the appropriate laws and rules of the road yet). Google Car has, at the time of writing, already been driven more than 1.5 million miles, and Google claims that the car can already detect objects up to two football fields away so the car can safely navigate around all manner of objects including pedestrians, stray birds, plastic bags flapping in the wind and, of course, other cars! As Google point out in their marketing material, just imagine the difference it's going to make to people when they no longer have to rely on their eyesight to get from A to B. It will mean a fundamental shift in people's ability to move around independently as they get older. With the demographic time bomb of a rapidly ageing population, self-driving cars have the ability to transform millions of lives. And Google isn't the only company working on them. The company getting most of the PR, both good and bad, is of course Elon Musk's Tesla. Pre-orders of the new Tesla have propelled the company into the record books for the highest value prelaunch of a product in history. Although the current cars aren't built to be driverless, it's been a key component of the Tesla vision.

And then there's Uber. CEO Travis Kalanick spent 2015 and 2016 recruiting a heavyweight team of some of the best and brightest people in the field of autonomous cars, robotics, and even some good old-fashioned car mechanics. Uber are serious about replacing its one million drivers with driverless cars. At the time, it seemed like an audacious (or even a little crazy) plan, but by the time you get to read this book, who knows? It might already be a reality. Things are changing fast – very fast. *Business Insider* recently predicted that there would be 10 million driverless cars on the road by 2020. But moving people isn't the only transport challenge that is on the verge of a massive disruption.

Disruption is coming to our skies too. There's strong evidence to suggest that the next big disruptive wave will be an exponential increase in flying drones. It won't be long before drones will handle most of our product deliveries and even have the capacity to provide much of the transportation and assembly needs to build roads and bridges. Amazon have been experimenting with drones for some time and Matternet, the drone network company, have a very bold vision indeed:

> Our mission is to make access to goods as frictionless and universal as access to information. Our products will enable people, companies and organizations around the world to build and operate drone logistics networks for transporting goods on demand, through the air, at a fraction of the time, cost and energy of any other transportation method used today. We are committed to building technology and products that can be adopted at a massive scale to serve everyone on the planet.[11]

Matternet is attracting serious attention. Mercedes have pledged a half-billion-dollar investment in creating a networked drone and autonomous van network powered by Matternet's technology.[12]

The thing is that we humans are astonishingly resource-hungry. With every development of technology that becomes exponentially better and cheaper, there are more and more of us that need to be served and maintained! The more efficient we get, the more efficient we need to become.

---

[11] https://mttr.net/company
[12] http://matternet.tumblr.com

Autonomous robots will soon be cheaper, safer, more precise, more predictable, and more reliable than humans can ever be, and this is going to have a big impact on our infrastructure. If we do the sensible thing and look to learn from Nature, then I believe that the patterns tell us that things will become less forced and more natural – if we let them …

In the near future our infrastructure will be more circular, just like the human body, a system that will run without the need of any steering from humanity. I believe we are on the verge of a set of complementary solutions that will allow our systems to produce their own energy. I foresee a system that will even be capable of being programmed to maintain itself.

We are seeing the start of automated shopping with the opening of the first Amazon Go store in Seattle. The new store has brought together the technologies of machine learning, computer vision, and AI, allowing customers to grab what they want and just walk out. No lines, no checkout, and no interaction at all. It's all done through the app on your phone and charged to your Amazon account. Amazon Go is looking to deliver total convenience and a much nicer shopping experience. They will, of course, also get a bigger slice of the money in your wallet by giving that to you.

The challenge with writing a book like this at this time is that things are moving so fast that predictions are becoming reality in weeks and months instead of years and decades!

Wave 2.0 Energy Generation and Storage Trends

Is solar improvement about to become exponential? The evidence is pointing that way. Today's solar panels are already ten times cheaper and more efficient than they were a decade ago and the rate of development has sped up significantly. Recently, MIT and Masdar Institute created a solar cell that's 35% efficient and less expensive than other supposedly high-efficiency cells currently on the market. Then just a few days later the Swiss Federal Institute of technology in Lausanne claimed it had gone one better by creating a solar cell that is 36.4% efficient. What's interesting from a growth wave perspective is that 36.4% efficiency is around double that of the efficiency of cells in residential use at the time of writing.[13] The plan is for a new company called Insolight to use the new technology and

---

[13] https://cleantechnica.com/2016/09/12/insolight-breaks-solar-cell-efficiency-record-hits-36-4-efficiency/

produce the high-efficiency panels and compete in the existing solar market.

The innovation and production of new solar systems is probably at a record high right now. There's a product called SolPad that is described by its manufacturer as 'the world's first and only truly integrated solar panel'. The product is one of a series by the Californian company, who describe their range as being disruptive energy products. They have a string of patents and have managed to combine the solar element with battery storage, inverter system, and intelligent software to create an integrated device[14] that gives people the capability to live off the grid.

Wave 2.0 Energy Storage Trends

Things are certainly moving quickly in the energy storage areas too; so fast that while I was still writing the final draft of this, Tesla just announced an update to the Powerwall home battery system, meaning that the new version can store double the energy of the first-generation battery and is around half the cost, plus it has an inverter built in this time, and Tesla claims that the unit needs no maintenance at all. It's fully automated and will be shipping before this book even hits the bookshops for the first time.

But although the Tesla product is a game-changer, it's still based on existing lithium-ion battery technology. There are other innovations in the energy storage field that are happening at the same time. For example, scientists at University of Central Florida (UCF) have developed a super-capacitor battery prototype.[15] They have shown that it can last up to twenty times longer than a conventional lithium-ion cell. According to Nitin Choudhary, a postdoctoral associate who conducted much of the research, the super-capacitors charge in just a few seconds, and that translates into you being able to charge your smartphone in a few seconds and not to have to re-charge it again for up to a week.

The new invention doesn't degrade, unlike typical lithium-ion battery cells that start a slow process of degradation after around eighteen months. In testing, the prototype doesn't degrade (unlike lithium-ion) and works like new, even after being recharged 30,000 times.

The difference is the way that super-capacitors store energy. They do it statically on the surface of a material itself. Traditional batteries rely on

---

[14] www.solpad.com
[15] https://today.ucf.edu/phone-charges-seconds-ucf-scientists-bring-closer-reality/

chemical reactions to store and discharge the energy. Using graphene as the material, researchers were able to create a large surface area to hold more electrons and increase the lifespan. Although the research is in its early stages it holds a great deal of promise. Just imagine what technology like this could do for electric vehicle ranges and a whole host of other applications.

Then there's the so-called 'gut batteries'. Using Nature as an inspiration, scientists have created a prototype lithium-sulphur battery with the potential of five times the energy density of a lithium-ion battery. What's so interesting about this technology is that it's able to mimic the structure of the cells inside our bodies that allow us to absorb nutrients in our small intestine. The proof of principle research paper, co-authored by Dr Paul Coxon from Cambridge's Department of Materials Science and Metallurgy, doesn't claim that the technology is commercially viable but does point out that the ideas have the potential to bring in a new generation of battery technology. Although this isn't the place to go into a great deal of detail about the chemical reactions involved, what's fascinating is that the researchers' new design makes use of a layer of zinc oxide nanowires. These nanowires are grown on a scaffold on top of the battery's cathode and the structure formed has the same shape as the villi of the small intestine. These little fibres are one of the key outputs from the chemical reaction taking place inside the battery and allow the resulting material to be reused. It's an idea in its infancy at this point, but what's fascinating is seeing how some of the technology is converging; in this case, energy storage and nanotechnology.

Overall, the trend is going the right way.

Bloomberg's New Energy Finance team estimates that price per kilowatt hour of power generated through solar will drop dramatically from $182 to around $132 by 2025. That's still high compared to the current prices of the carbon-based alternatives, but what's important here is the trend. What the evidence is telling us is that with the amount of research and development that's going on, and our collective will to preserve our planet, that it is almost certainly going to be renewables and off-grid technology that will be powering our world. It's not just going to change the way we power things either. It's going to shift the power base of entire states and nations who have based their wealth and economies on fossil fuels. Now that's more than just a technology shift; it's going to shift the entire global political system.

Wave 2.0 Water Trends

The ability to produce water from air is a rapidly developing area of technology. There is a recent invention called WaterSeer that is a small water generator that can produce up to eleven gallons of water per day by extracting water from the air using the difference in temperature between an above-ground turbine and a collection chamber installed six feet underground. The invention is aimed towards areas of water poverty and has a first-generation price tag of around just $130.

Then there are bigger capacity systems already coming to market. A great example is the prize-winning SunToWater system that won first prize in the 2015 Impact Challenge from Singularity University. This is a much bigger capacity water generator, supposedly capable of producing between 40 and 100 gallons of potable water per day. The technology is different as it works by using a combination of salts to pull the moisture out of the air, fans, solar heat (which pulls the water out of the salt), and a condenser (to extract the distilled water for use).

Then there is a solar panel system called Source, developed by Zero Mass Water,[16] a start-up with a mission to 'democratise drinking water', which turns water vapour in the air into clean, drinkable water. With roughly ten per cent of the world's population lacking access to safe, clean drinking water, many of these innovations could hold the key to solving the massive challenge of how to overcome the problems of poor infrastructure and the resulting issues like disease and drought. There is a future on the horizon where there is clearly the potential to no longer rely on government-provided water systems. Just image how the world would be impacted if access to clean water was genuinely democratised.

What's interesting here is that much of this technology is getting closer and closer to mimicking how nature works. The biology and technology parallels are striking and they will only help to serve us and take our technology forward.

So what would it be like to live in a world where some, or even all, of these technologies were part of our everyday experience? Come with me, and let's walk into a day in that future.

---

[16] http://www.zeromasswater.com

Chapter 24

Living in a Wave 2.0 World

Imagine you wake up in the year 2030 and you look out of your window. What would you see, feel, and experience?

Well, first of all, I believe that everything we do will be sustainable and circular. Nature never wastes anything, and all material moves through a lifecycle of usefulness. I'm feeling confident that the technology and communications systems we are developing right now are going to help us do the same.

Our technology (inspired, in many cases, by Nature herself) is going to help us work out how to do it, and the communication networks (already proven to mirror nature) and the virtual elimination of language barriers will allow us to communicate the critical importance of the changes right across the planet. What's going to make the changes stick is our fundamental willingness to do it, and that can only happen if we share the ideas in every language.

So, welcome to 2030. We have stepped into an era of hyper local and recycling. A focused realm where your own personal 3D printer to your local production hub can produce everything you need, from the clothes that you wear to the electronic devices you use.

Even the vehicle that you drive (or fly!) will probably be produced in your own local town. Many of the products in your home have been designed and co-created by open-source communities. That's why they are so good, and why they get even better at lightning speed. Gone are the days from the early twenty-first century where millions of versions of the same product were released to great fanfare on the same day. Remember that? When smartphone batteries caught fire and millions of expensive centrally produced valuable products became virtually worthless overnight?

The products you use today are constantly evolving and improving in digital form so you request the changes you need, and hey presto, the adaptation is done. The things you need are now downloaded from the web as an intelligent design file and can be 3D-printed on demand. 3D printers (these days more accurately called 'materialisers') are now a mature technology and are able to print all kinds of materials, including your food! The 'ink' in your printer comes in many different forms and you can load cartridges that contain almost everything – from transparent and fragile glass to super-strength titanium. Even flexible, synthetic plastics, rubber, or biodegradable organic materials can be loaded up. Materialisers are able to 3D-materialise or grow a wide range of materials on a molecular level, like metals, wood, plastics, carbon, and even entire electronic circuits and families of newly engineered super materials like graphene. When we 3D-materialise a biodegradable material or product, we can already even programme on a molecular level when the material or product starts to deteriorate and returns to its natural form. We have struck a perfect balance of recycling and materials reuse at last.

Products and materials can now be grown on a molecular level and with a molecular precision. Every material structure we can imagine can be created with a 3D materialiser. 3D materialisers can materialise almost every product you can imagine: electronic devices like smartphones and wearables, clothes, furniture, food, spare parts, bikes, and even entire transportation vehicles like cars and drones, including all the electronic circuits that are necessary for these to function. The packaging, where needed, can also be materialised – but we don't need much packaging anymore because most of what we need doesn't have to be transported over long distances.

Nearly all the things you need day-to-day, even new internal electronics for your smart devices, can be printed entirely at home. If you aren't sure how to assemble the printed parts, you don't need to worry because your trusted home robot can do it for you. Or, if it's something that was printed in a local hub in your village or town rather than at home, there's a smart network of drones or autonomous vehicles that will drop it to your door. It might even deliver itself! There's very little waste either, because old products are recycled by robots locally and ground materials are extracted and reused as printing filament for 3D printers. Missing or unique ground materials for 3D printers are shipped in by drones, and autonomous transport vehicles form other production hubs. In addition, technology has transformed from hard, cold, and often unnatural-feeling devices to more natural-feeling devices that perfectly adapt to human needs. Advanced machine learning tools have helped us to unravel many of the mysteries of nature, allowing us understand and mimic nature on a deeper level, ensuring two key things:

1. We will be able to create a new generation of technology that is more organic and feels more natural to us, and
2. Because we can see what a miracle we have been blessed with, we are looking after it better every year.

We are going to be powered in totally different ways too.

Our Energy Infrastructure in a Wave 2.0 World

By 2030 we are likely to be running on a distributed, decentralised, and circular energy infrastructure. Technology allowed us to understand the energy generation and storage systems that nature designed so beautifully.

Because we were able to get some new ideas and fresh thinking from things like photosynthesis and the respiratory systems of nature, our new energy systems work in an entirely circular way and so, just like nature, they are highly efficient!

In our natural world there are two important types of cells that help to produce and store energy; they are the chloroplasts cells (which use carbon dioxide and produce oxygen and glucose) and mitochondria cells (which use oxygen and glucose and produce carbon dioxide). Within this pairing, both types of cells feed on the waste product of the other, so they work in a fully circular way. It's an incredible system and the ultimate in intelligent design of perfect balance.

With the introduction of cheap and affordable bio-solar panels (light energy that fires up chloroplast-type cells) with integrated bio batteries (chemical energy that fires up mitochondria-type cells), our modern homes in 2030 convert light particles (photons) into cheap electrical energy on a local scale. Genius! Our modern integrated bio batteries enable us to generate energy in the daytime and store it until we need it at night. We can now use energy 24/7 without burning polluting fossil fuels. These bio-solar systems are nothing like we used in the early days of solar power; these new units are highly efficient and therefore very compact.

The small bio-solar unit on the back of my house is enough to power and heat my entire family home. When it gets to the end of its natural life, I just nip down to my local 3D materialisers at my local production hub where they have one 'growing' ready for me. It's a very cost- and robots powered by artificial intelligence and are mainly responsible for the heavy industry tasks like mining, extracting, and breaking down the raw building materials so that they are ready for use as filament material for our advanced 3D printers. The focus is now on small, localised production hubs that are able to produce a wide range of products. We can programme materials to fall apart after a certain period of time or after a specific trigger signal, so these products or materials are easier to recycle. Every new product will be designed and built following the cradle-to-cradle principle. Advanced product design tools that use smart machine learning technology are able to design very complex products with optimal strength and with the minimal use of materials, just like Nature does with bone structures. Because we are now able to create products and materials on a molecular level and in batches of just one, waste has been reduced to an absolute minimum. Almost every product you ever use is created on demand.

Our Transportation Infrastructure of the Future

Even though fewer and fewer goods need transporting large distances, some products and building materials are transported through a highly efficient logistics network. Once again, we had the foresight to look to Nature's incredible designs and take inspiration from the highly efficient transportation system in our own bodies.

We used the amazing designs of our organs and vascular network and learned how to model them to create a sophisticated transportation infrastructure that delivers what we need on a 'just in time' basis. In the last decade, smart sensors and devices became so cheap that we started to put them in almost everything. Now our devices are so small, we simply print or inject them into the packaging of any cheap retail products. This is what started our revolution of smart, connected devices in the packaging of almost every retail and consumer product.

We can now know everything that goes on during our logistics process and can plan for things like: temperature, GPS location, speed, delivery date, product age and quality, sound exposure, chemical exposure, radiation exposure, and even G-force. Less and less gets damaged or wasted and the information is always available to the logistics network. Our modern network of billions of interconnected logistics (the internet of things) is now producing massive amounts of data that can only be governed and controlled by artificial intelligence in the cloud.

Our highly effective transportation system uses a massive network (a fleet that behaves more like a flock) of autonomous transportation vehicles (drones, pods, cars, trucks, trains, boats, and planes) that is also controlled by an artificial intelligence that is aware of every tiny detail that is happening in the entire global logistic network. All the autonomous transportation vehicles and the products and goods they transport are part of a big, interconnected network full of smart sensors and devices. Every package is aware of its start location and its end destination, and the package itself will choose the best and most efficient modality to travel to its end destination. Our logistics system handles physical packages just like the internet is handling virtual data packages; packages always take the most effective route to their end destination. When a package is lost or defective it will be replaced by a new one immediately. Our entire transportation system operates almost fully autonomously; like the organs and vascular systems in our body run on a subconscious level, our logistics system/network takes almost zero human attention to work properly. For the secure management of all the logistic data we use a kind of smart blockchain system that keeps track of every transaction within the network. Even at the production phase, products are already programmed for a specific end destination, and if there's an incident that means products don't arrive at their end destination they automatically return home!

The need for physical transportation of people is also different than a decade ago. Now, because most public transportation vehicles like private cars, taxis, buses, and trains are fully autonomous and don't have a human driver, the number of fatal accidents has been reduced dramatically. We have new methods of transportation like ground pods and air pods. These are small cabins that you can sit in that take you to your destination via the ground or via the air. They are like small unmanned drones that are able to transport people over short distances.

2030 Waste Management Infrastructure

Nowadays ownership of things isn't as popular as it used to be, because with ownership comes responsibility, maintenance, and replacement when the thing stops working properly. As we live in a world where products have an average life cycle of months or weeks instead of years or decades (and that's okay because most things just get reabsorbed and materialised anyway), it's hard to own things, because you are always having to let them go!

So we have turned into nations of sharers. We share more and more physical products within our communities and own less 'stuff' than we did just twenty years ago.

New technology platforms make it very easy to purchase and share a complex product part-time or based on a timesharing principle with the rest of the community. You don't want to own a car anymore, you just want to use one when you need it. You don't even want a lawnmower, you just want a pretty-looking lawn.

The Future of Physical Display Products

The introduction of incredible photoreal mixed reality devices, which project light particles (photons) directly into your retina-enabled technology to project realistic and interactive virtual 3D objects into your real environment, made a lot of physical technological devices obsolete. For example, around 2025, television and computer screens became virtual screens directly projected in your eyes, and many of the physical hardware devices that controlled our environment became virtual. The screens of tablets and smartphones is now directly projected in your eye, and the processing is done in the cloud, so they became obsolete a few years ago now.

The Future of Food

Biotech enables us to grow our own healthy foods within our home or local community. Food does not have to travel all over the world anymore; it's all grown and consumed locally. Any packaging that is used to protect our food during transport is biodegradable. Thankfully, obesity problems were largely solved when personal nutrition and portion calculations came in. It's almost hard to remember what it was like to eat until we were full, because these days portions are adjusted depending on our body measurements, metabolism, and our physical activity. As a result, we don't use more than we need, we aren't getting overweight, and our healthcare costs have dropped dramatically.

For the waste that still happens occasionally, we have a 100% recycling record. Our 100% water and air is purified using naturally inspired systems, all our packaging is biodegradable, and our vehicles are powered by sustainable and renewable power. A flock of autonomous vehicles collect the waste materials and take them to a local recycle unit. No human attention is needed in this process.

The Future of Our Healthcare Infrastructure

We have entered a time of unprecedented health. The expensive and inefficient healthcare infrastructure that was mainly focused on treating symptoms was wiped out a couple of years ago now. The traditional big pharmaceutical companies and medical mindset was often focused on earning money and avoiding liabilities, but not on healing people in the long term. The management of these companies knew they could earn more money from sick people, even though the doctors and medical staff themselves were doing their best.

Thankfully, as a global community we have seen the light. Although there are still some elements left of our traditional healthcare system, it's mainly focused on fixing acute and life-threatening health problems that are, for example, caused by accidents or ageing.

Our old system was pretty good at this stuff, and since the massive changes and our ability to manage our food and therefore our own health, and the ability to 3D-print drugs, we have been able to put the talent of our doctors and nurses to better use. Advanced technology like sensors and artificial intelligence are now able to diagnose the root cause of our symptoms and cure our body faster than ever. We are now only interested in the root cause of health problems and we now have technology that helps us to find that root cause. Smart sensors and artificial intelligence provide humanity with the tools to monitor and predict our individual health and our level of well-being. Cheap but advanced sensors in our clothes, jewellery, wearables, sport accessories, homes, and cars measure everything and report back to our AI, doctor, or health community professional if we need to get checked out!

The Doctor In Your Pocket

In future, you are going to have sensors that have the capacity to help you to stay healthy. These sensors will be able to measure everything from your location and speed of travel, right through to small and very subtle biological processes and information patterns going on inside your body. They are so sensitive that they can, for example, diagnose diseases from only the smell of your breath or your skin. Once again, Nature showed us the way here because it was discovered late in the twentieth century that dogs (who have a truly amazing sense of smell and a massive portion of their brain dedicated to processing smell) could sniff out certain cancers.

Modern sensor technology was inspired by examples in Nature to look into our body using ultrasound frequencies and analyse our blood and DNA without sticking a needle into you!

Machine learning algorithms have identified many subtle information patterns and structures in our body and they have also identified many root causes of diseases and can come up with information patterns to heal our body on an information level. As a result we now have information medicines (bio-electric medication) that work in the electromagnetic/light spectrum instead of the chemical spectrum like traditional medication did in the past. With this powerful new technology we are able to reprogramme our cells to help us cure almost every chronic disorder or disease – disease that is less prevalent anyway because we are managing our health better and are subject to fewer pollutants than we were thirty years ago. We have bio-electric medicines, which are electric information signals that instruct our cells in our body to relax, recover, and regain health, restoring the health of our entire body. These virtual medicines are shared freely over the internet; they are like free, open-source software programs, and many of them aren't patented and free for everyone to use without cost or licence. Everybody in the world with a smart communication device and internet connection can download or stream these information medicines from the web and use them to regain health. These informational medicines can be given to our body using our smart communication device and in some cases with the use of an extra accessory. Now that's what I call a useful app!

Our smart communication device (I'll call it a smartphone for simplicity's sake, but in reality it's way more than that!) acts like a real-time biofeedback device that can measure our health and in most cases heal/correct it directly without needing a visit to a doctor or medical specialist. Based on the measurements, our smartphone asks you some additional questions, like an old-fashioned doctor would. All the input is gathered and compared in real time with hundreds of millions of other similar cases. The artificial intelligence behind it comes with a diagnosis and possible treatment within seconds. We are living in an age where almost all chronic health problems can be prevented and restored by the use of smart devices and smart e-health technology. In the world of 2030, our primary communication devices are also the devices we use for treatment on a personal level. Also, our homes are full of wellness technology that monitor and correct our living environment in real time. This wellness technology controls and regulates air humidity, air pollution, noise/sound pollutions, EMF radiation, and many more environmental pollutants that may be harmful for our well-being. These same wellness devices are also present in all of our transportation vehicles and public buildings. Everything is assured to create the most healthy and comfortable environment for people, animals, and plants.

resource-effective process, meaning that people in all parts of the world can make use of it – almost for free. The units can be created in many forms and integrated in many building materials so integration is almost seamless and invisible. Bio-solar technology can even be used as a transparent, glass-like coating that covers the surface of an electronic device or transportation vehicle. So it can also be used to power mobile devices and public transportation vehicles and even our entire industry.

The wave of innovation that brought us the widespread introduction of bio-solar technology also fuelled a fast-growing network of peer-to-peer access internet points that brought free internet to all the corners of the world. Simply by 3D-materialising and placing another bio-solar-technology-powered access point the network was expanded almost without any limitations and it changed the entire world economy. The balance of power shifted from central governments back to local people again.

The beauty of the new system is that the bio-solar access points generate and store their own energy and can therefore operate independently of any infrastructure. Internet signals are transmitted wirelessly so are very cheap and reliable. There's a blockchain-style network that was built in the early 2020s that now covers the entire world. Governments didn't want to do it because it threatened their hold over their populations, but the visionary entrepreneurs stepped in, paid for it, and saw results and massive change in a very short space of time. In the end, the power bases shifted, and there was nothing that any of the old-style power brokers could do about it.

The New Age of Production Infrastructure

Remember the days when things used to be produced in large, centralised production facilities called factories? These days, they are almost a thing of the past. The only large production facilities that are built brand new are built in a way that is more like the organs in our body; they are sustainable, self-sufficient, and fully support a circular ecosystem. We are the most incredible machines, and thankfully we learned a few years ago how to replicate Nature's processes in ourselves, and scale it to do other things. We learned the precise processes that the organs in our body use to serve the community of cells that makes up 'us'. We discovered how our body breaks down raw building materials into nutrients that can be used as building material by the individual cells.

What is left of 'old-fashioned' factories are now run almost entirely by

Chapter 25

Wave 3.0 – The Future of our Information Infrastructure

Wave 3.0 is the Communication Wave

It is a basic human need to communicate. It is a basic need of all life to communicate. As you already know, it's the power of our communication systems that drives our ability to survive. Whether that is a series of cells inside the human body communicating to request water or nutrition, or a nerve pathway helping the brain move the limbs to help us run away from danger, communication is at the heart of everything.

Communication also ensures that what's needed across the different parts of any community can be delivered. Our need to use our auditory and visuals senses to get a clear picture of the environment is one level of our needs. We also need to connect on an emotional level too.

Remember Maslow's pyramid? The third layer of human requirement is love and belonging – and it's a direct connection to our Wave 3.0 developments and the need they serve. That's because Wave 3.0 is all about connecting.

In the natural world, Nature has a certain predictable way she goes about creating bigger structures, and it's a very information-hungry process. What started in the early days of evolution as simple nerve nets around the mouths of early animals to help them hunt more efficiently, eventually evolved to become the senses that we enjoy today – hearing, feeling, seeing, tasting, smelling things. Just like in our technological world, in the beginning, cellular communication was local too, but as Nature pushed through its own waves of innovation, the communication systems got better and better. Our cellular mobile networks did the same.

On a human level we see that exactly the same process of development happened in the early days of mass communication. We started with the telegraph, which enabled small networks in local areas. Our point-to-point connectedness improved, and we could telegraph over longer and longer distances. We invented the fax machine (remember those?). Fax seems like ancient technology now; out of the ark, in fact, and yet I have baby boomer friends who remember very clearly their introduction and how fax revolutionised our business communications.

Now we have phones, microphones, cameras, and sensors that are able to gather some kind of information from the real world and transfer that into the digital telecommunication network.

So in the same way that Nature helped organisms to build more complex nervous systems, we did the same!

The MRI scans of our own neural networks look remarkably similar to the patterns of our physical communications networks like our telecoms systems and the internet.

We can compare that with local area networks that first started in universities, for example, where multiple computers or devices were connected to each other. Later on we also saw that universities and companies were connected to each other, and they were growing backbones. Now we have very big backbones between America and Europe, and big countries, and big data centres.

We developed cable networks, intercontinental and global cable networks and transatlantic cables that allowed America to communicate with Europe. And later still, we had fibre, radio waves, and routing distribution centres that distribute all the data to the right places. That's just like the early animal life and their early 'nerve nets'. The parallels go on and on.

That's no accident, but nor was it quite deliberate design. It just so happens that communities of cells, and communities of humans have the same problems to solve and the same solutions to solve them. It's inevitable that we came up with similar patterns to solve the problems.

As each wave creates a launch platform for the next wave to form, it's like a rocket with multiple stages, where each stage adds speed to the speed the rocket already has. With the easy distribution of energy and people through the processes of Wave 1.0 and 2.0 industry, businesses went global and expanded very quickly indeed. The ability to talk to people in previously far-flung places without actually going there (thanks to Alexander and Mabel) only served to speed things up.

Our world has become bigger and smaller at the same time.

If you want to sell products in a global economy you need to have a global communication channel to tell your potential customers about what you have to share with them. The need for a fast and reliable information and telecommunication infrastructure that re-connected humanity was born with Bell and transformed with television. 600 million people tuned in for the moon landings. Yet it started with the very small beeps of the telegraph. Eventually I believe that our communications will grow into some kind of quantum network where we can transport huge amounts of real-time information that enables us to see and experience all the places of the world (and our universe) from the comfort of our own chair at home.

Today, we can already live-chat through our social media channels to anyone else just about anywhere else in the world. More on that later, because social interaction is becoming a bigger and bigger part of our future.

So What's the Next Big Communications Shift?

Our next communication challenge will be to connect the billions of people who still don't have access to the internet.

Once again, just to confirm the idea that we are transitioning to 'The Age of the Entrepreneur' (where billionaires replace government functions), in 2016 there were some interesting developments on expanding internet access.

Mark Zuckerberg, Facebook's founder, announced he was bringing together a project team (even including some of his biggest competitors) to solve the challenge of communities and countries that didn't have the resources to get everyone online. Zuckerberg and his highly creative collaborative team have some radical and disruptive ideas to make it happen, from supplying satellite internet stations connected by lasers to solar-powered planes that fly above our weather systems to provide the technical capability to deliver bandwidth to outlying communities.

Once again, an approach that comes from a disruptive generation has now actually become part of the establishment itself. That life force is now changing the landscape of a globally connected world faster than has ever happened in history before.

How Technology Will Help Us in the Future

At first, we created simple human-to-human communication networks, starting with lighting fires on hillsides and sending smoke signals between villages, then the telegraph, and then the telephone. After that we got radio too, and that satisfied our auditory senses. Later, the next revolution was television (and later video), and that satisfied our visual senses. The large cable networks that distributed those moving images throughout the community gave all of us a better understanding of our environment, and that meant we started to get more environmentally aware. Fast forward to today, and that 'television' is now in our hands in the form of a smartphone or tablet computer and the lines of 'TV' are increasingly blurring as tablets get smaller and phones get bigger.

The cable networks are now as fast as the wireless networks that move large amounts of invisible data through the air. If something happens on the other side of the world we now know about it within seconds. Some of our biggest news stories now break on platforms like Twitter. Our smartphones are our ears and eyes. We use them to experience the world in high-definition audio and video.

Right now, as you are reading this, a couple of billion of users just like you have access to the internet, and amazing things will come from that.

But what happens when all of us are connected to the internet? What happens when millions of people suddenly have a voice? What will be the result of millions of creative minds all having the wherewithal to invent new services, apps, and products? How quickly will we progress then?

You can see why I believe we are moving into an exponential phase of creativity and change.

What is going to happen when everyone has access? Just imagine what progress we can make when everybody on earth has access to free education, healthcare, and advanced knowledge. It's those important questions that people who have power, reach, and influence in today's world need to spend time carefully considering. The old style of controlling populations won't apply soon. They just won't work anymore. Everything is going to change. I spend every day looking forward at the trends and playing scenarios forward to see how they might change our future. We are moving into interesting times. Our technology is going to give millions of people incredible power and it's up to people with a conscience to provide the wisdom for the technology and knowledge that flows from it to be used as a force for good. Now is not the time to abdicate and surrender to the tide.

Chapter 26
Wave 3.0 – Trends

One of the hottest trends that we see on an information level is the rapid increase in bandwidth. We already have proven 5G wireless transmission and that is predictably doubling in bandwidth every couple of years. It started with 1G, 2G, 2.5G, 3G. Now we are at 4G, and that's a common network speed.

5G is being introduced in 2017 in the Netherlands. In the near future there won't be a difference between wi-fi or other bandwidths or wireless protocols, because the device itself will be choosing the protocol that suits, and you will have, always and everywhere, the connectivity you need. We are moving towards that very quickly indeed.

Currently there are large parts of the world, such as large sections of Africa and India, that don't have a good infrastructure, mainly because many of these countries have an agricultural background and large rural populations, but as you have already read, changes are coming here too. That's going to change things for all of us because the populations in these areas are massive, and up until now have been seriously under-represented. Many so-called Third World countries don't have internet backbones or optical fibre running through the ground but we know that won't be necessary in the future. The entrepreneurs are seeing to that by looking for solutions from completely new technology. What Facebook and Google are doing by providing free internet in many countries will change the world for all of us. The technology behemoths may sound altruistic, but there is always a price. When all those new users start using the Facebook- or Google-provided connection, they're also giving their search preferences and personal information away.

What we will see in the next few years is that more and more parts of the world will be connected, and that the price of the internet becomes a commodity. Now these days you pay $30 or $40 to have internet connection. In the near future I believe that the price will drop dramatically, and eventually it will be almost free for everybody. There are already signs that governments are planning exactly that and starting to make progress to bring access to more and more people. For example, late in 2016 the European Commission announced a plan to provide free wireless internet access to every town and village in the EU. Although at this stage their goal is to make it available in public places they describe as 'the main centres of public life' it's a good start. New York has already rolled out a similar idea by creating a series of hubs across the city. Despite the resulting social challenges that they unexpectedly ran into, it's further evidence that the authorities are recognising digital as a utility rather than a luxury.

What we'll also see is more and more of the smart sensors we talked about earlier. In the early days, I think it's likely that we will see them appearing mainly in the healthcare sector. Eventually, we'll see them in all kinds of wearable technology. More and more of these sensors will be implemented in more and more devices. For example, in smartphones there are a lot of GPS sensors, temperature sensors, height sensors, air pressure sensors already. These are going to become so cheap so quickly, and get so small, that every device that has a power voltage connector will also be equipped with more and more sensors. There is already technology in development using artificial intelligence and mobile technology to collect the largest amount of voluntarily gathered health data probably ever collected. It was crowdfunded and has attracted the leader of the President Obama campaign, Scott Thomas (and his entire team), to move to Silicon Valley and take the project further. They are already seeking FDA approval for their vitals app and urine app to help you take control of your own health signs. Times are changing fast ...

In addition, we're going to move faster and faster towards an internet of things (IoT), where everything is connected. From your health signs to what food your phone orders for you, it's all going to talk to each other and make intelligent decisions for us.

What Maturity of Wave 3.0 May Look Like ...

When every device with all its sensors and inbuilt intelligence has the capability to talk to all the other devices we will have reached Wave 3.0 maturity. That maturity point is going to create an immense amount of contextual information.

Our technology will know everything about us: which room you're in, who you are with, where your car is, where your clothes are, whether your refrigerator is empty or not.

A lot of these 'things' are going to be talking to each other, and I believe that this will create a kind of 'ultimate knowledge', where everything will be registered and talking to everything else.

With the right algorithms and machinery algorithms we can do a huge amount of good with all that data. Eventually what we'll also see is the blockchain principle being introduced for more and more information sources.

What the blockchain basically does is to re-distribute the power of the network from the power of the few (those in control of the network itself) to the power of many.

Another big trend that is going on right now is that people are taking control of the internet again. Large corporations and governments may own the internet right now, but the question is this: for how long can that be sustained?

Today our internet is ruled by a couple of powerful organisations that distribute the DNS (Domain Name System), the URLs (Unique Resource Locators), and the domain names. That's going to change, I believe, and the process has already started. We will have a more evenly distributed power base running the web. In October 2016, the US government handed over control of the World Wide Web's phone book to the non-profit organisation ICANN. With various stakeholders from governments, representatives from private companies, and internet users from all over the world, ICANN now has direct control over the Internet Assigned Numbers Authority (IANA), the body that manages the web's DNS, meaning the US government has finally released its grip.

There was a recent funding pitch on the crowdfunding platform Indiegogo for a home server product called Daplie that was over one thousand per cent overfunded. Daplie claimed to allow users to centralise their entire digital life. The powerful pitch included the idea of being able to 'Take Back the Internet':

Take back your photos from Dropbox, take back your phone from iCloud, take back your email from Google, take back your social network from Facebook, take back your Digital Life from these 'Internet Kings'. Cloud lets you literally put back the 'I' in Internet.

It's already happening out there on the so-called 'dark web'. From there, people are spreading new software that you can install on the router in your home, and that connects to the router of your neighbour, which in turn connects with the router of other neighbours. It's likely that what we are seeing happening on the dark web is the beginning of a consumer-level network that's independent of the large distribution centres run by the government and large corporations. That's a trend that's likely to continue.

Trend – Miniaturisation & Audible Computing Convergence

Just as the smartphone is becoming an essential part of our lives, there is a new question being asked by the digital trend-setters: what comes next? Well, according to IBM and one of their external partners, Bragi, the next transformational technology set to transform our workplaces could be audible wearable computers small enough to fit into your ear.[17] Bragi already have what they have called a 'hearable' on the market. Their product, named The Dash, is marketed as being the first truly wireless hearable and has biometric feedback built in, and gesture controls. The tie-up with IBM is looking at combining that with access to IBM's Watson, with the first applications likely to be workplace usage, and IBM is talking about making the technology 'more natural, interactive and convenient'. What I think is so interesting about this commercial R&D pairing is the increasing convergence between related software, AI, and hardware partners. It's suggesting an ever-greater convergence of companies that will propel developments faster than ever before.

The Rise of Cognitive Computing

This is an area that's growing at an unprecedented rate. So what is cognitive computing? Well, it's all about finding a way to mimic how our brain perceives, understands, and acts on things. Where traditional computing has focused on rational and analytical computation, the new generation of computers is likely to be more like us. We humans just don't work in such a linear way; ask anyone who has tried to understand the demands of a complex personal relationship! The more subtle aspects of how we live are powered by our more intuitive right-brain functions. The scientists who are developing these new cognitive computers are looking for ways to recreate those skills.

---

[17] http://www.digitaltrends.com/cool-tech/ibm-watson-bragi-the-dash/amp/

For example, IBM has developed a neurosynaptic chip that's been designed to model the neutrons and synapses of a human brain. That's a massive shift from the way we have been building computers for the last seventy years. The early chips have millions of 'synapses' and only turn on when they are needed rather than running all the time. Of course, IBM aren't the only commercial big gun in the game either.

In November 2016 Hewlett Packard Enterprise (HPE) released a press release[18] about a new proof of concept prototype of what they call a 'memory-driven computer'. HPE claims the computer has speeds up to 8,000 times faster than a traditional computer and uses photonics (light photons used to communicate across the chip on a nano scale), just like our brains.

Is Computing About To Go Quantum?

The rise of quantum computing is something that many figures in the technology industry are watching very closely indeed. But before we talk about what it is, let's look at why we might find it useful and what problems quantum computing solves. First of all, the excitement comes from the fact a quantum machine has the potential to perform an exponential number of calculations simultaneously; for certain types of challenges that opens up new horizons of scientific discovery. One of the limitations of our current classical models of computing is that it's based on a binary system (in essence, our entire computing power on the planet is currently powered by a simple system of 1s and 0s – an astonishing thought in itself when you consider the richness and complexity that a binary system has given us), and that means to do massive numbers of calculations you need a very big machine indeed. And big machines need power; a massive amount of power.

To give you an example, at the time of writing, the biggest classically built computer based on the traditional binary system is named Tianhe-2 and is located in China. This monster of a machine uses enough electricity to power 20,000 households, is roughly half the size of a football field, and contains 3.2 million Intel cores. In an attempt to regain the USA's supremacy in the high-performance field, Barack Obama claimed that

---

[18] https://www.hpe.com/us/en/newsroom/news-archive/press-release/2016/11/ 1287610-hewlett-packard-enterprise-demonstrates-worlds-first-memory-driven- computing-architecture.html

America would build something billed as an exoscale computer that would be thirty times more powerful than the Chinese machine. Not only that, but he claimed that it would be done by 2020. It's a nice idea, but it has a flaw. And the flaw is a pretty big one because, with current technology, it will cost a billion dollars to build and will need an entire nuclear power plant to run it!

So now you can see why the race for what's being described as 'quantum supremacy' is on. Put simply, it's a race to prove that a machine is indeed operating using the principles of quantum mechanics, where binary calculation is old news and bits become qubits (or quantum bits) that can scale exponentially.

It's a hugely exciting field and there are currently three main players: Google, IBM, and a Silicon Valley start-up called Rigetti Computing.

The well-respected technology author, founder of the X-Prize and co-founder of Singularity University, Peter Diamandis, refers to quantum computing as being a 'sixth paradigm' technology,[19] not just because of the fundamental change in the way it works, but also the incredible potential it offers to solve some of the biggest problems of all. With Google and Rigetti both claiming that they will reach quantum supremacy within eighteen months, the opportunity to crunch enough data to be able to look for patterns is phenomenal. Quantum computing[20] and the ability to do millions of calculations simultaneously would help us gain a greater understanding of complex areas such as climate research, cancer and medical research, materials technology, life sciences and biomimetics, energy systems, photovoltaics, and more in a remarkably short window of time compared to the computing we have available today. It's one of the most exciting areas of computer science.

So what would it be like to live in a world where some, or even all, of these technologies were part of our everyday experience? Come with me, and let's walk into a day in that future.

---

[19] https://singularityhub.com/2016/10/10/massive-disruption-quantum-computing
[20] https://youtu.be/g_IaVepNDT4

Chapter 27

Living in a Wave 3.0 World

Imagine you wake up in the year 2030. What might our tele-communication infrastructure look like? There are some signposts from Nature already present, and study into the area of the 7 Waves of Innovation give us a peek into the future.

I believe that in the future, the majority of our communication infrastructure will be distributed, decentralised, and dematerialised. I think our research will have taken us to the point where most of the information we want to exchange travels using frequencies that are in harmony with (and not harmful to) organic life.

By 2030 our network is based on a grid, or a peer-to-peer structure.

That's a form of network where every internet-connected device is also an access point for other devices in its surrounding vicinity. The advantage of peer-to-peer information grid technology is that people can now connect every corner of the globe to the internet. The cost and effort is minimal and the need for physically demanding and costly infrastructures will have evaporated.

Remember that we used to have big, centralised energy-wasting data centres? Not anymore. By 2030 they are a thing of the past. Most of the computing power and storage is now distributed and done by a network of bio-solar battery-powered quantum computers. It's not just that the technology we use today is powerful; it's also compact. There's massive power capacity housed inside something not much bigger than a small twenty-first-century refrigerator.

We modelled the new communication infrastructure on the elegant system inside our own body. Our very own backbone infrastructure (our central nervous system) connects our brain with the rest of our body (via our peripheral nervous system) so our limbs know what to do.

So our 2030 communication infrastructure also has a backbone that connects the fast and computing intensive neural networks that power multiple artificial intelligence applications. These are the 'brains' that run and oversee our society, legal, traffic, companies, and logistic processes, and much more. It turns out that after some of the concerns about AI were addressed by the leading minds of the day in the early twenty-first century, our AI quantum machines have turned out to be one of the most important parts of our infrastructure.

Our Society Runs On Artificial Intelligence

These cheap and redundant AI quantum units process Yottabytes[21] of data very efficiently and around the clock. They work tirelessly 24 hours a day, 7 days a week, 365 days a year. Our modern quantum computers use very advanced 3D chips that are working on a molecular level, and we build them from completely new and superconducting materials only discovered because we had the combination of innovative creative thinking and the computing power to design them. These backbone server grids use bio-inspired structures like spiderwebs or mathematically beautiful honeycomb structures that are able to process extreme amounts of stress. And where there is more stress the networks reinforces itself automatically, just like bones in our body. In the human body, where there is the most pressure our bone structure responds by increasing bone density and becoming much stronger as a result. When humans worked out that we had all the answers inside us, around a decade ago, the speed of development went exponential.

We developed routing systems that were powered by artificial intelligence and had the processing power to make sure that stress on the system is now automatically and evenly distributed over the grid and not focused on one central point.

At the end-user level the internet is organised just like our peripheral nervous system; the internet is even more decentralised and distributed, and every internet-connected device is also an access point that acts like an amplifier, router, and storage device all in one. That's how our global access to the web has improved so much so quickly. It's also why the internet is very scalable and resistant against defect modules and parts. If a node in the network is broken it is simply bypassed by other nodes in the grid;

---

[21] Definition of Yottabyte = Giga Terra → Peta → Exa → Yotta

simply place a new part in it, and it completely reconfigures itself to work properly again.

Almost every internet-connected device (and there are trillions of them in 2030) has multiple sensors that act like senses for the bigger system. The more sensors and the more powerful AI we develop, the more humanity as a whole is becoming aware of its environment and what is happening in every corner of the world. Just like an organism that has many and accurate senses, the internet is now fully aware of its environment. When living, organic organisms are fully aware of their environment they adapt to that environment much better and faster and have a higher survival rate. The internet (the nervous system) and all of its connected devices (equivalent to our senses) are now doing the same thing for our humanity. The internet is not connecting cells – instead it connects humans and technology, and it prevents humanity from harming itself.

How do We Pay for All This?

By now most of the transactions on the internet are made using the blockchain principle. That was technology created back at the beginning of the twenty-first century. It was the very start of a commercially viable 'cryptocurrency'. Later, with the wider introduction of blockchain for many online transactions, many of the middleman-type functions in our economy got wiped out. The clever ones saw the writing on the wall and transferred their connections by becoming platform hosts instead.

These days, secure transactions of any kind are made between individuals, and not between individuals and large corporations. The introduction of blockchain a few years ago made a lot of physical products much cheaper. And with the added advantage of the revenue going to the creator of the product (instead of the bank, reseller, or big middleman organisations) it became commercially viable to be an inventor or producer again. Back in 2016 Apple's App Store took 30% revenue of every product sold. Amazon also was able to get hefty commissions.

That middleman economy was called out by a writer, Douglas Rushkoff, who wrote a book back in 2009 called *Life Inc: How the World Became a Corporation and How to Take It Back*. Rushkoff pointed out that, at the time, only around 20% of the price of almost any product was real value and the other 80% was either margin, profit for banks, returns for hedge funds, logistics costs, retail markup for trading company's or production companies. He predicted that if there were no more middleman companies, products would be much cheaper. He predicted that if products only cost 20% of the price we see, we only have to work 20% of the time (equivalent to one day a week) to fulfil the same needs. Blockchain enabled much of this to happen in recent years.

How Advanced Sensors Have Changed Our Lives

Just like a living organism develops more and more senses to increase survival rates, humanity is developing more and more sensors to get a more accurate perception of the world we live in. Today, in 2030, we have trillions of connected sensors that give us very advanced and sensitive 'senses'. Our sensors have allowed us to make extensive use of autonomous vehicles (cars, drones, trucks, trains, etc.). They are packed full of sensors.

Our homes are full of sensors. Our clothes and communication devices are full of sensors. Our infrastructure is full of sensors. In fact, almost everything man-made is equipped with smart sensors.

Our modern autonomous vehicles all have sensors, and our communication devices and wearables sense everything in detail going on around each of us. So everything that's happening outside on the street is part of the information going back into the system. All the smart devices we use in our homes sense everything that is happening inside our homes and public buildings. The type of sensors that we have in 2030 are so sophisticated they are able to register all kinds of information. These sensors are able to register much more information than we can now imagine. We have sensors that can gather data even around the entire light spectrum, the entire sound spectrum, all kinds of radiation, very subtle vibrations, energy patterns in the human body, complex information patterns in our brains, material properties from a distance, electromagnetic forces and disturbances, gravity and G-force, and many more.

The quality of the sensors that are around us every day in 2030 is remarkable. It's the unique combination of sophisticated sensors with the AI in the cloud that processes the information the sensors gather that allow them to artificially see, hear, smell, and feel like humans – only better! What do I mean by better than us? Well, modern sensors can smell many times better than our dogs, see a detail from a distance better than an eagle, and hear many times better than a bat. They can even register the earth's magnetic field many times more accurately than birds do.

For example, the many cameras in your home and car are so

sophisticated they can measure your heart rate and blood pressure from a distance.

The smell sensors in your clothing and your bathroom gadgets are so sensitive they can smell any kind of disease from your breath in a very early stage.

Sound sensors can recognise you by your unique breathing pattern from a distance and can analyse your voice and vocal tones and find, for example, health problems or nutrition deficiencies. They can even measure your voice stress levels and remind you to calm down!

Spectrum analysers in your communication device can see exactly what nutrition and ingredients are contained in the meal you're about to eat. These sensors are so smart, so they don't even send all the data through. They are bright enough to send just the filtered conclusions that are useful for the next layer that processes the information. Your home sensors are even equipped with small integrated neural network processors and local AI to process the information locally. This reduces the noise in the rest of the internet. Still, all these sensors generate unthinkable amounts of data, because there are so many! All this data and information from these sensors is monitored and processed by artificial intelligence. In this way, humanity has access to absolute knowledge of almost everything.

Humanity Knows Everything – But What Will We Learn?

Most of the data and information is transparent, open, and accessible for everyone. We long ago found an agreement that balanced openness and privacy, although we need to continue to be vigilant so that we maintain a healthy balance of cost and benefit to each individual and to society as a whole.

Ultimately, the more we share data, the more our community and environment can benefit from it.

Future of the Internet

It is 2030, and these days, most of the world's population is connected with each other via the internet. The only people who are not connected to the internet are the ones who actively choose not to be; to live 'off the grid'. By the way, the internet in 2030 does not look anything like the internet did in 2016. The internet is not an image on the screen of your desk or an app on your smartphone. The internet is everywhere around you; it is completely immersive and it blends in naturally with your environment. The internet is like an additional reality on top of our physical reality. It's an immersive reality that touches all your senses and it feels just as real as our physical reality. Most of the time you experience the internet blended with our physical reality but sometimes, if you choose to, you can become completely isolated from our physical reality and step into virtual reality.

What's Real in 2030?

It is very hard to tell where our physical reality stops and where the blended reality starts. The bandwidth and speed of our communication infrastructure has grown exponentially in the last two decades. If you would have asked someone in 2016 to describe the internet bandwidth and speed we have today, they would have been speechless. They had no language and measures that would have done the job of even describing it back then. So yes, things have sped up!

The internet is everywhere and always available, and it helps humanity to unite and act like one organism or system that is aware of itself and protects itself. We use the internet for everything now, but it's great to be able to say that we don't suffer from an information overload anymore. That's because artificial intelligence searches and filters relevant information for us and presents us with exactly what we need to know at the exact moment we need it, and always in the right place.

The information we need is presented in a natural, intuitive, and visual way, so we don't have to internally translate the information we receive. It is directly processed by our visual cortex. Now, that's what I call progress ...

You – As a Hologram

Our communication device has become a very important and virtual extension of our body that connects us with the rest of humanity. We got a preview of that back in 2016, when every teenager in the land was perpetually glued to his or her smartphone! Now, we are all glued to them – we just don't have to physically hold them anymore. They are part of our everyday experience. Our modern communication devices present information in a highly engaging and visual way and we interact with these devices in a very natural way, just like we interact with other people in normal life. When talking to other people, we see them in front of us in real size and indistinguishable from reality. It is like talking face-to-face in real life. It's like FaceTime used to be, just full-size and in 3D. And because our devices monitor our eye movements, emotions, gestures, facial expressions, heart rate, breathing, body temperature, and other body information, they can make an accurate and holographic representation of our entire body in real time. The hologram that is you now follows all your movements, expressions, breathing, eye movements, and more. It's like you are really there – at the other end of your device. Communicating with people on the other side of the world is like talking to someone in the same room with all your senses involved. Human-to-human communication in this way feels like telepathy; it really feels like magic when you talk to a holographic representation of a real person for the first time.

The 2030 Communication Device

Now you even have (as do most other people in the world) a personal holographic communication device (the HCD replaced smartphones about five years ago). It feels so different interacting with your HCD now because it feels very intuitive and natural. The device itself has almost been virtualised and dematerialised and instead of a lump of something we need to carry in our pocket, our HCDs are much more stylish. The ones due out next season include HCDs hidden as part of stylish glasses, fashion, and even jewellery. Modern HCDs project light particles right in your eyes, and as a result you see virtual reality holographic 3D objects projected and blended seamlessly into your physical reality. The projections are so real that sometimes you can't even distinguish the difference anymore between holographic objects and real physical objects, unless you choose to. These holographic objects vary, from virtual monitors and TV screens that display practical information to thirty-metre-high dinosaurs that walk in your backyard just for fun. We can interact with these virtual objects like they are real objects, but with the endless extra interaction possibilities that virtual objects provide. The best part of these communication devices is that we don't communicate through these devices like we did with our smartphones in the past, when our smartphone screen was the medium. These new HCDs let us communicate with other people around the world as if they are really next to you in flesh and blood so the device itself (technology) is not standing in between you anymore.

I believe that it's when technology becomes natural like this that it will have the biggest impact on people and society. The communication devices render a complete holographic world on to our physical world that people can only see if they have their device enabled. This holographic world can be universal, or tailored completely to individual needs and preferences. For example, through these holographic devices you can see buildings that are not there yet or people that are virtually visiting your town from the other side of the world.

Telepathy is Here to Stay

I think it's likely that within five years from 2030 our HCDs will have advanced to such a point that the neural sensors will be able to read patterns in our brains and even read our thoughts.

From that moment on, as a race, we will have the capacity for brain-to-brain interfaces with a much wider bandwidth than every other device in history. That's going to enable us to communicate on a thought level. It's going to feels really liberating because you are now able to communicate on a level without any language, symbolic, or technological constraints. What freedom that could bring.

Of course, the first version of this thought-powered technology has its limitations but these are nothing compared the limitations we have when we use language, text, images, or holography. These devices work in two directions, so we can receive information and send information using thoughts. With this new technology we are now also capable of controlling robots with our mind – the robot body will feel like it is our own body and our brains will adapt very quickly and easily. We can control humanoid robots with our mind; you are going to have to get used to it, but after a while you are going to be able to do amazing things that your own physical body just wouldn't be able to do. With this type of device and control over projecting your own thoughts you can do things like connecting to a drone in a faraway place. Imagine feeling like you are inside the drone on the other side of the world. You could explore, for example, the Grand Canyon, with the drone that's packed with sensors and a 360-degree view of the world sending you such ultra-realistic images and sounds and feelings that you are really 'there' (at least as far as your brain is concerned).

Beyond Holography

Communication processes were already very efficient using holographic technology but with the use of thought-powered technology, misunderstanding other people becomes a very hard thing to do. The linguistics don't get in the way anymore and intent is embedded into all our communications. Trust is easy to give (and easier to withhold from people who don't deserve it). These thought-powered communication devices will unite humanity like no other device has ever done and will bring us all a giant step closer to one single harmonic and coherent community. We have the opportunity to act like one organism in our collective best interest. Now we have the technology to make it happen.

Chapter 28

Wave 4.0 – The Future of Automation

The Biggest Data Challenge In History

You've had a glimpse of the possibilities that come from Wave 3.0 technologies, so now it's time to move into Wave 4.0.

You already know that:

- Wave 1.0 is about survival and multiplication
- Wave 2.0 is about the infrastructure and the security that is needed for the next phase of growth
- Wave 3.0 is about networks and communication systems

So what's Wave 4.0 all about? Wave 4.0 is all about solving the problems created by the massive amounts of data produced in Wave 3.0.

Now, with the new volume of information, just moving the data around the system isn't enough anymore. Now there's a new problem: there's literally too much information. There's so much data, so much to think about, and so many decisions to be made as a result of the constant data flow, that it's now essential to automate things. If that doesn't happen then the whole system would collapse and shut down under the strain. It doesn't matter if 'the system' happens to be a single human body, a community of people, a community of cells, or an IT network. The effect of not automating an ever growing 'network of things' is a level of complexity that creates a catastrophic overload if a solution isn't found. That solution is automation. Putting some elements on autopilot so that conscious thinking doesn't need to take place based on every new input. A little bit like you don't have to think about how you brush your teeth – you just do it, on autopilot. You don't think about how to drive your car – you just drive and have some mental bandwidth to notice hazards and plan your next holiday while your legs and arms do the work of controlling your car without you really noticing the detail.

Think about the growth of our telecoms. Wave 3.0 did a great job to generate our advanced communication and information networks and there were huge amounts of information flowing over those networks. That was great, because that's what they were designed to do – move huge amounts of information around.

There were positive side effects of ever growing amounts of information to move around too. It created a new demand for electronic devices that were able to process more and more information. There were tube and transistor powered radio transmitters and receivers, satellites with integrated circuits, and other mechanisms that could process all that telecoms information digitally.

The next phase was (and still is) a constant drive for miniaturisation that pushed more and more information processing power into increasingly smaller areas. The integrated circuits became so advanced that entire logic systems could run on a single chip, and then CPUs appeared and computer manufacturers made devices that became even more complex to operate, and they really were the preserve of businesses and enterprise. The only individuals that had access to computers outside the business world were located in universities and research labs. They were the original geeks.

In 1980 something changed dramatically: computers became personal, and the personal computer business and business automation exploded. Bill Gates was instrumental in making computers personal and Steve Jobs was obsessed about usability and great design. In many ways, they were both pioneers of Humanification before it even had a name. They both made computers more human. That was the start of a massive shift in the day-to-day 'value' of technology to ordinary people. The name 'personal computer' was a stroke of genius. It made Bill Gates the richest man in the world for a time, and Steve Jobs' vision helped Apple ripen into one of the wealthiest companies on the planet. They were true pioneers and had the vision to take more and more of the processes of computing and make them invisible to most ordinary users. That was all only possible because the software revolution allowed so many basic computing functions to run in the background, allowing the user to only concentrate on getting the result, and leaving the machine to carry out 99% of the processing for them. That's a great summary of what Wave 4.0 is all about – it's all about things going 'unconscious'. That's simply a process of automation, and that applies from when you are driving your car and talking to the person next to you while you eat a snack (I'm not recommending driving distracted, but accept that people do it every day and our brain is capable of multi-functioning) to the app on your phone reminding you about your upcoming appointment. It's all there, running in the background, leaving your conscious processing power to do the work that's at the front of your mind.

So, on a physical level, Wave 4.0 is all about building operating systems and automating things. On a social level, that means sharing control. A great recent example is the Information Communications Technology (ICT) automation revolution that started in the 'eighties, progressed in the nineties, and continues now.

Nature Showed Us the Way

Following through on our theme of using Nature to help us see the patterns, let's view Wave 4.0 and take a look at how Nature solves the complexity problem that Wave 3.0 created.

For creatures with nervous systems, there's now a massive amount of information moving around from all parts of the organism and a need to process that information to make some sense of all the data. So organisms developed a brainstem, or reptile brain, a very basic brain that's able to automate all the biological hardware that's under it.

The brainstem takes over much of the co-ordination that the animal needs. It becomes the conductor of the orchestra, so to speak. The conductor automates a few things so that he can leave it running while he pays attention to coordinating the orchestra rather than playing the instruments. The brainstem is then able to manage the heart rate of an animal or an organism, manage the visual input, process auditory input, decide what needs to happen as a result of the tactile input, and give also output to the muscles or the motor divisions that respond to the data. In other words, it's Wave 4.0 technology that keeps the tune playing in the background while life rumbles on.

We did basically the same as we developed our ICT technology. At first we started to develop computers based on relays and tubes. Later, our computers became smaller and smaller. We reached the point where we moved on to integrated circuits where many thousands of transistors are packed on a single chip. Those chips evolved and evolved to core processors and eventually CPUs, where millions, or hundreds of millions, of transistors are packed into one single small area.

Those incredible chips enable us to process lots of information that's flowing on our electrical circuits and through our information and telecom networks. And all that creates a new challenge. When you process information, you also need some kind of memory.

Memory – The Next Big Enabler

Just in the same way that animals need some sort of memory (so they don't need to re-invent a new strategy to find food every time they get hungry), our ICT processes needed memory too.

We solved that challenge with simple repeatable processes and specialist memory hardware. Maybe you remember the early floppy disks, working memory, and hard drives in the early computers. Those technologies stored short routines that could be used later on in a process.

Memory Enables Repeatable Behaviour

When you can save temporarily to short-term memory, you can reuse it later. That basic idea is the key behind behaviour. It's simply a series of pre-programmed reactions laid down inside an operating system of some kind, and it applies whether it's animal, vegetable, or technical.

Another thing the simple 'reptile' brain was able to do was to process visual information. At the start this was very simple processing because scientists believe that the first animals with visual capabilities only had the capacity to see dark, light, and to detect movement using the contrast between the two.

These very simple visual receptors may have been simple in engineering terms, but the brainpower needed to **process** the information is massive. It was a challenge in brainpower terms for early animals, and our technology also mirrored the same challenges.

That's where our early man-made technology struggled; not in creating the machinery to 'see' things, but to process the 'seeing' into useful data and be able to put it to good use in the right way at the right moment. We just didn't have enough memory capacity to do that until recently.

As Nature's creatures' eyesight got more sophisticated, the light receptors in animals' eyes evolved to feature receptors of a much higher-resolution and eventually to camera-like eyes with a lens and a visual retina. Their brains also adjusted to that growth of visual information by developing more processing power. In other words, as sight got better, the brains got bigger too. Early organisms started to create or develop a visual cortex. That's the part of the brain that can process all that detail; and you need massive amounts of paired-up processing to process visual information. It's very processing-heavy indeed.

So it's clear to see that, in essence, people and the computers we use have evolved in roughly the same way. That's because, from an information perspective, we are built the same way because we faced all the same information challenges!

When we first started working on computers that could 'see', our technical wizards and programmers started by building 2D graphics cards that offered the equivalent of simple black/white/contrast vision.

Those clever people later moved on to create 3D graphics cards that had the power to 'see' and process incredible amounts of parallel information. As memory capacity grew, so the sophistication grew and the graphics grew with it, and that in turn created a demand for ever more sophisticated graphics.

Eventually these kinds of processors evolved in a perfectly natural way to become graphical processing units (GPUs). It's interesting to note that it was these GPUs, with only marginal modification, that were later used to run machine learning algorithms' neural networks.

Back to Nature again, because she still has plenty to share with us. As animals started to develop their visual cortex (an amazing structure in its own right) to meet the processing needs of all that visual input, the animal was learning more and more new things. It had this huge parallel processing machine now embedded in the brain.

Now we see exactly the same type of progress happening in the field of man-made technology and AI. A decade or so ago we started to develop GPUs. Now, Google and Nvidia are using those same processors to run massive parallel processing power for their neural networks and the machine learning algorithms that drive the technology you and I take for granted every day.

So, let's bounce back to Nature again for a moment. As well as just a visual cortex, creatures also develop a brainstem to automate lots of different functions. It's automation on a large, organic scale. The brainstem of any creature (including us) controls the autonomous functions of the body it's there to manage; it controls blood pressure, heart rate, and all the internal processes in the organs, and a whole lot more. In human terms, you could say that we have a built-in operating system!

Think of our physical body as our hardware, with a software layer that sits on the hardware, and the job of the software is to automate all kind of processes below it. Our brain is the ultimate piece of hardware, with the brainstem and visual cortex the top of the range software.

As we learn things that both help us and harm us, we write programmes (learned behaviours) and run those programmes over and over again. It doesn't take many repetitions of the programme to almost hardwire those behaviours into automated reactions and processes that we can run over and over again to increase our chances of survival.

Computers Have Drivers – We Have Instincts

There's also a remarkable parallel between our automatic reactions and the way computer drivers work. I doubt that anyone thought about our evolution when the early hardware and software engineers were grappling with the challenge of getting our early computers to talk to the printer. And yet, once again, the common-sense pattern of evolution kicked in. In the early computers, you needed to install different drivers for all different kinds of hardware. A driver (or device driver, to give the full name) is simply a group of files that enable one or more hardware devices to communicate with a computer's operating system. It's basically a mirror of the same process that happened in biological history too. After early evolution, there was a development of core reflexes and instinctual behaviours. That was when Nature started programming living things so that when a specific trigger, impulse, or stimulus fired off, the organism reacted in a predefined way. That's what we collectively refer to as instinctive behaviour.

When we think about how that compares to technology, there are some obvious equivalents. For example, the first personal computers that you could buy were pre-installed with applications or an operating system with applications on it (like word processing, spreadsheets, etc.). There wasn't a choice about how they worked or what they did; you couldn't change them. They were predefined applications. They simply processed information in the same way every time, but they did make things simpler. That is so like the simple behaviours of the first animals; the behaviours worked just like early IT applications.

An important part of evolution for animals was the development of increasingly precise movement. Creatures started to develop motor functions with muscles and tissues with the ability to contract and relax. That gave the ability to move and to propel the creatures forward. In tech terms, we watched as the early robots (mostly simple electrically powered arms and devices) automated all kinds of processes in our factories. Those early robots were only possible because of what had happened in earlier waves. Before we built the robots, we had built the technology networks and cable networks, and then on top of those we designed the chips that did the processing and so the level of 'intelligence' gets higher and higher. Each layer makes the interface more simple to use, and the next stage of development is then possible.

I believe most of our economy, of our governments, companies, and people are in the Wave 4.0 layer of development. It's a selfish period in our evolution. We have evolved to the point where we know that we can automate most of the processes that help us survive. Nature did the same with the brainstem to create a selfish brain that automates the processes in the body and helps to survive. That's the reason the selfishness is there; it enhances survivability so it's a very important trait that's inherent within all of us. Our personal survival – and the survival of our genes through our children – is paramount. That trait has flowed through our society and become the main driver of many companies, governments, and organisations all over our world.

Our next big challenge is to go to the next phase and to become more social. It's not going to be easy. We have layers and layers of protection to keep the system stable – stability that now poses the threat of becoming our undoing if we don't move forward and upwards into the next Wave 5.0 – the social wave. But before we get to that, let's pause for a moment and look at the Wave 4.0 trends that are happening, or I believe are likely to happen over the horizon, and even take a peek at some of the trends that are here already but aren't mainstream enough to have been noticed yet.

Chapter 29
Wave 4.0 – Trends

General Trends

In the future it's likely that computer processing power and storage will be almost unlimited. In addition to that, you are going to be able to access just about everything from just about everywhere.

I predict that hardware systems and operating systems that we see and touch on a daily basis will become more and more invisible for the end user. The user interface of our technology and computers is going to become so much more natural that our interface with our machine world will become blurred. It won't be long before it's going to be hard to tell the difference between reality, virtual reality, and fantasy.

Electronic devices with microchips and sensors inside are going to keep getting smaller, cheaper, and better, with the next big trend being the development that pushes things to get so small you get into the realms of nano-scale devices.

I believe that we are getting really close to a point where we won't even be able to see most of the technology anymore. Tech is going to be integrated inside all kinds of other things, like glasses and even in our clothes.

When it comes to storage and processing power, you are going to see these becoming more and more distributed. You will see less and less on your device and more in the cloud.

So instead of your pictures being on your smartphone, you will be cloud-based and your device will simply function as a method of retrieval. You are also going to find it harder and harder to pinpoint where certain data is stored or processed.

Right now, most of the network and cloud solutions are stored on big server parks from Amazon and Google. Eventually the individual level of processing power which consumers have will be so big and so fast that you will be able to tap into other people's technology memory sources; your devices may become useable by others too. You could be sharing a massive network with your neighbours.

Another trend is translating more and more digital information to visual information in an increasingly immersive 360-degree virtual reality. There are already lots of new devices popping up that are able to translate data into a virtual experience that is so real and so responsive, it's become hard to differentiate between what's real and what's virtual. It's another mirror of what happened in the natural world. When the first animals had a visual cortex they got a richer and more detailed experience of their surroundings. The better they experienced their environment, the better they adapted to that environment, and the better that was for their survivability. We now see that happening in our lives too. The more processing power and the better the visual graphical representations of a virtual environment we get, the better we can experience that environment, the better our survivability is in that environment. It's helping robots to operate in environments that are too dangerous for people to work in.

Another big trend that I can see coming is that every technological device will have its own operating system. We now have a few large operating systems – Android, Apple, and Windows – but in the future (and, in fact, it's already happening) every kind of device, your coffee machine, or your refrigerator, your car, every kind of technology, will have its own operating system. The goal of that is to automate that piece of technology to the point where we can interact with it without even knowing how to control the technology itself.

Think of it like a complexity extraction layer.

More and more apps will be developed automatically. If you have some kind of challenge or problem, then a computer program that you can talk to will solve that problem for you by creating some kind of app. If and when the problem is solved, then the app won't be necessary anymore and it will dissolve itself again automatically. That's virtualised solutions becoming more and more like an organic being or material of some sort. Once it outlives it usefulness or comes to the end of its natural life, it breaks down and gets absorbed back into the earth. Ashes to ashes. Dust to dust. Idea to ether. Pixel to pixel.

We will be able to talk to our machines so we won't see apps or interfaces, we won't notice the operating system interfaces, or even notice our communication with our technology. You will be able to talk at a really high level with machines. That is going to feel more and more natural.

Dag Kittlaus, co-creator of Siri – itself a spin-off product born at the Stanford Research Institute (and later acquired by Apple and incorporated into the iPhone), has founded a new company, Viv, that takes the interaction into a conversation and claims to be more natural than Siri, with a massive shift towards more natural interactions coming from a new era of dynamic programme generation (or, put simply, software writing itself). Kittlaus gave a confident demo[22] of his new intelligent AI platform at the 2016 TechCrunch Disrupt event, where he talked about Viv becoming 'the intelligent interface for everything'.

So, Humanification is coming, and it's coming very quickly indeed. Every week a new voice-operated device comes out, and every day the machine learning embedded in such devices makes us feel more at home with the technology. The devices get smarter, and we get more used to it being that way.

And talking about being at home, what about the robot that can cook a Michelin-starred meal for you? Sound tasty? Mark Oleynik of Moley Robotics designed a kitchen with robotic arms that learned how to cook, taking their lessons from top chefs. The robot 'learned' by repeating every movement made by the human chef. With one recipe, master chef Tim Anderson cooked while the system recorded every motion, nuance, and flourish and then replayed his exact movements through the robotic hands. Bingo. It might not be long before you can download a recipe, order up the pre-measured ingredients, and let the robot make your meal for you.

So when it comes to Wave 4.0 automation trends I believe we are only just at the beginning of that S-curve; there's way more to come yet.

Wave 4.0 Automation Trends

Wave 4.0 – Autonomous Production and Handling

There are some great examples of how many of the ideas I'm sharing with you are already a reality, even if they are currently only in their infancy.

---

[22] https://techcrunch.com/2016/05/09/siri-creator-shows-off-first-public-demo-of-viv-the-intelligent-interface-for-everything/

In August 2016 the BBC (British Broadcasting Corporation) reported the story of a very lucky lawyer and his Tesla car.[23] Joshua Neally was driving his Tesla Model X home from work from Springfield, Missouri, to his home in nearby Branson when his normal drive home took a bad turn. After he had pulled on to the highway, Neally was struck by a piercing pain in his chest and stomach. Instead of calling an ambulance, he tasked his car with finding a hospital, using the Tesla's self-driving mode. Roughly 20 miles (32km) later, the lawyer's Tesla arrived at the road leading to the hospital emergency department. He later told the news site *Slate* that he manually steered the Tesla into the car park and checked himself into the emergency room for treatment.

Then there's the Baxter robot from Rethink Robotics, a company who talk about their robot being trainable (as opposed to programmable). Baxter robots have a range of fingertips that the company claims can 'feel' different objects that used to be difficult for robots to handle.

The YuMi robot from the industrial giant ABB is designed to work side-by-side with people. And then there is the massive rise in the use of industrial drones that are now active in fields as diverse as farming (checking on livestock), hard-to-reach oil and gas rigs and pipelines (monitoring infrastructure), search and rescue (including thermal cameras), and security services. Boston Dynamics are developing robots with astonishing qualities, including some almost spooky human physical characteristics, and recently broke the record for land speed with their Cheetah robot. Their BigDog robot is one of the most advanced all-terrain robots on the planet at the time of writing, and is visually like something we only imagined and could see using special effects in movies until recently.

Amazon have already automated distribution centres, with over 30,000 robots scuttling about. In a move that could have been seen as predatory, Amazon CEO Jeff Bezos was so convinced of the massive advantages that robotics were going to bring to his company, he dug into his cash pile and pulled out a cool 775 million dollars to purchase the main global supplier of distribution robots, Kiva. For a time, it put the users of distribution centres into a total spin until some new suppliers had chance to catch up. That bold move gave Amazon a significant business advantage for a while, and the opportunity to grab a big market share while its competitors faced a gaping hole in the market where Kiva had been.

---

[23] http://www.bbc.co.uk/newsbeat/article/37009696/tesla-car-drives-owner-to-hospital-after-he-suffers s-pulmonary-embolism

Then there's the future of autonomous logistics – it's already taking hold, and the developments in this area are currently having a long-awaited surge.

On 7 December, 2016, a bag of popcorn and an Amazon Fire TV stick left a warehouse in the university city of Cambridge in the UK. Just thirteen minutes later, both items were accepted by an Amazon test customer. Amazon posted a video showing a fully autonomous drone taking off from the warehouse and flying over fields to deposit the package just outside the customer's home. There were no humans involved. Although this was a very small trial, Amazon has stated its intention to expand the trial to hundreds of users very soon.

Then there's a company called Starship Technologies, who provide what they refer to as 'the new bot on the block'. The Starship robot is built for hyper local deliveries; it's basically a very clever lockable box on wheels, whizzing everything from takeaway foods to books around, and even helping you get your shopping home.

The Daimler Freightliner Inspiration is a new breed of autonomous truck, and the Freightliner became the first licensed autonomous commercial truck to operate on an open public highway in the United States. Then there's Ehang, the Chinese-manufactured drone that's been created to transport people, and we couldn't talk about infrastructure without mentioning Google Car, Tesla Autopilot and Uber's autonomous system – all examples of massive disruptive technology which is either here already or about to become part of our everyday lives.

So, as you can see, the future of autonomous transport is here already. Sooner or later our governments and regulators are going to have to catch up. *Business Insider* recently predicted (based on documented increases and mathematically calculated estimates) that there will be more than 10 million automated vehicles on our roads by 2020. Now, that's one big shift.

Another trend that is worth watching is how nanotechnology is going to influence our chip technology. We are already seeing a new way of using carbon to create complex structures that will give us the possibility of bendable computers, meaning the development of truly wearable technology. IBM is experimenting with growing carbon nanotubes using the model of how Nature grows crystals. It gets over many of the challenges of working with the materials that have, to date, held back scientists from exploiting the massive potential of true miniaturisation.[24]

---

[24] https://futurism.com/ibm-has-devised-a-way-to-grow-computer-chips/

Chapter 30

Living in a Wave 4.0 World

By 2030, it's likely that technology is going to be so cheap, powerful, and easy to adapt and integrate that there are no valid reasons not to automate! Almost every job, routine, or task that is in any way boring or not worthy of our attention will almost certainly be automated. That's just the surface. Look deeper into the trends and what's going on now and map those to the predictive patterns of nature, and this is what you will probably see in the future.

Intelligent Operating Systems Everywhere

By 2030 I believe that almost every piece of IT hardware will have its own operating system, because the hardware layer below will become so complex and advanced it will need an abstraction layer to connect, communicate, and socialise seamlessly with all other IT devices in the internet of things.

It's going to be an inventor's dream because technology is probably going to be sophisticated enough to allow everyone who has even basic tech skills to build as many technological applications and devices you want yourself.

I predict tech will get modular. Parts of solutions are likely to be traded and exchanged like building blocks. Creating tech solutions as a social pastime won't just be restricted to the geeks! When that happens, progress will explode.

Welcome to the Material World

Let's imagine for a moment that we are already in 2030. Today, it's normal for many types of sensors and chips to be materialised in a moment (that's the 2030 equivalent to 3D-printing) using generally available materialisation devices. If the job is too big or too complex for your materialiser at home, then the materialisation device available in your local production hub can cope with the job. Materialise a new car? No problem!

That same technology has allowed so many new pieces of IT hardware to be developed every single day. On a daily basis, enthusiastic and creative people inside communities get to invent things, do a rapid prototype, and bring them into use.

Thankfully, in 2030, we aren't reliant on the big dinosaur companies of olden time to do this for us anymore. We can move much faster than they ever could. We do it today by working as a team that comes together to solve a problem that matters to us locally. Local challenges, local communities, local solutions; and when we find something that we think could work on a bigger scale we tell other communities about it and we all knowledge-share.

Almost all of these new hardware devices we create together are unique due to the hardware structure being completely new because each creative mind that comes to the challenge has a fresh perspective. Plus, a big contributing factor to that is that today's operating systems are equipped with a layer of artificial intelligence. That means they are able to adapt to almost any new technology hardware layer below. Our modern, intelligent, and adaptive operating systems can learn and adapt to different types of technological hardware. The AI sees the structure of the hardware technology, investigates on its own and discovers what it can and can't do. Then it creates a specific 'driver' for that peace of hardware or technology. We learned a long time ago that when programmed with enough flexibility and machine learning capability, our technology acts in a similar way to a child when it's given something new like a bike, a new toy, or a gadget to play with. It doesn't take long for the child to discover what the hardware can and can't do and rapidly learn how to use it.

In 2030 it's not just smart electronic devices that have their own operating systems: it's also bigger things like cars, trucks, drones, and flying vehicles. The operating systems in these vehicles take care of all the technology in the vehicle and how it blends seamlessly into the bigger logistics system. This allows all the vehicles to move like one system without any internal congestion. Back in the early twenty-first century they used to queue up with traffic at peak times. People used to spend wasted hours sitting in traffic! Now, the vehicle operating system (OS) is always communicating with the bigger cloud-based OS, and that has enough intelligence and processing power to coordinate all the other vehicles in the area.

Our Intelligent Homes

Even our homes now have an operating system. It's so normal that we don't really notice them because they are so sophisticated. Your home OS detects and connects all the technological devices in your home. Your home sensors, robots, lights, energy system, wellness devices, and all other appliances and communication devices all talk to the AI-driven intelligence of your home OS.

Your house will even know who is at home and who is out and what you are doing, and can even predict your next move. That's why service at home has got so good! Your home OS remembers how you like the settings for your lighting, sound, acoustics, music, and even the decorative effects and can fit them perfectly for your mood on that day.

But what happens in a 2030 house when you aren't alone? Well, when multiple people are in a room your home OS has the brainpower to create an environment setting that works best for everyone in the room, and here's the fascinating thing – when people are happy, the social interaction is so much more fun because everyone is in a better mood. Teams work better, people enjoy the company more, and it leads to more cooperation, common ground, and better emotional health. Technology isn't just about getting things done; it's about making things better and sometimes the differences can be subtle but incredibly powerful.

The Future Of Our Shared Spaces

I predict that all public buildings and 'offices/working areas' are equipped with their own OS, managing and serving all the needs and preferences of all the people who are in them at any one time. Our future workspaces are going to be able to give us exactly the right environment for the job we have to get done.

Companies (here in 2030 we now prefer to call them productive communities) also have an operating system. Instead of a traditional management team, these communities run on cloud-based operating systems that co-ordinate all the tasks and people in a coherent way that's the most efficient way of doing things, using people who are best suited to the tasks that need doing.

I foresee that by 2030, these cloud community operating systems are even capable of coordinating and orchestrating communities that could contain a million people or more who could come and work together seamlessly to complete complex projects or tasks.

The first cloud community operating systems that worked this way were online platforms like Quirky, Airbnb and Uber, which coordinated millions of people be able to coordinate projects and ideas in real time. In the future, I believe that even entire countries will be able to run on these kinds of cloud operating systems. There will be millions of specialist online platforms that coordinate and automate all kinds of processes and coordinate millions of people in real time – and they will probably be able to talk to each other! These cloud operating systems will have the capacity to learn from all the interactions and optimise their own performance 24/7/365.

If these cloud operating systems sound far-fetched, it's no different from how the early reptilian brains worked. They also coordinated and orchestrated millions of organic cells in a harmonic and coherent way. Nature did that millions of years ago. It doesn't take as big a leap of imagination to think that we will be able to do the same for millions of processes with the computing power we are developing now.

2030 Human-like User Interfaces

By 2030 I predict that communicating with machines/computers is going to be as easy as communicating with other people. The user interfaces that we will use to communicate with machines are going to become so natural it won't even feel like you're operating a machine anymore. You are going to be able to use your voice, gestures, and probably even your thoughts to communicate with machines. Almost everyone will be able to access any kind of information and control advanced exponential technologies.

No Language Barriers

You are going to be able to talk in any language to a machine, and it will understand you without any delay or struggle. The signs of real-time translation were well under way in 2016 and it's now a technology that we are all familiar with to the point we don't even notice when someone else's mother tongue is different to ours. By 2030 machines will be so powerful that they will be able to fully adapt to humans instead of what happened earlier in the century where we had to learn to adapt to our machines. This means that everybody has a simple but advanced interface to control highly advanced technology. You won't need to be a programmer to create advanced digital products, services, and solutions anymore. With your personal communication device on your head you see direct visual feedback projected in 3D right in front of you.

The End of Loneliness?

If you communicate with an artificial intelligence, you can choose to see a human-like character projected in front of you that has a voice, shows emotions and gestures, and has its own unique character. If you find that creepy, you can change the character. You'll be able to carry out really in-depth conversations with these AI assistants about anything you like. Thanks to fast machine learning algorithms and the exponentially increasing amount of data about yourself that you'll be generating each day, these AIs will learn how to communicate with you in such a personalised way that you'll probably swear it's your closest friend. Imagine an AI buddy who will incorporate your fantasies, ideologies, preferences, choice of linguistic styles and slang, your favourite topics and content, and even insider jokes into your 'personal' conversations. These AI-powered assistants will probably end up as a combination of your life coach, your personal teacher, your personal trainer, your mental coach, your personal doctor, your personal lawyer, your personal private banker, your trusted counsellor, and personal negotiator.

The Future of Applications

So by 2030 there will probably be so many of these intelligent operating systems with high-level user interfaces that most simple apps will become obsolete. Intelligent operating systems are able to generate software routines (apps) on the fly; based on your needs, a specific app is created and this app will only exist as long as you need it. Ashes to ashes.

Imagine being able to tell your house that any time you get home after dark you want the lights to go on, the curtains to be closed, and to have music playing that perfectly fits or lifts your mood at that moment. From then on, your intelligent operating system does this for you the moment you walk in the door. That's a big shift from where we were in the early twenty-first century, where we could do most of these things electronically but needed a different app for each one.

Apps are Dead – Long Live Apps

For specific and specialised tasks there are probably going to be apps that are still readily available. Think for example about creative design apps, specialised communication apps or entertainment apps. In the past, applications or apps were simply fixed software that ran a specific routine for you. You downloaded an app, and from time to time the developer sent you an update that upgraded the functionality or safety of the app. In the future, the rise and effectiveness of AI means that the apps themselves will be able to constantly adapt to their environment and rewrite themselves to meet the needs of the user.

In 2030 apps probably aren't going to be static anymore because they are effectively just algorithms stored in the cloud and they can be accessed by everyone. Apps like this will be in a state of constant flow, meaning that the code is upgraded in real time by self-learning systems. As the software code of the apps we are going to be using is probably written by machines and constantly updated to meet the needs of the users, the new job of the creator of an app is simply to create a framework of functional modules (algorithms) based on the needs of a specific user. The visual user interface will be tailored for you because every user is unique. The user interface learns from the user and adapts if needed. That's already happening on our social media platforms. We all see a totally unique version of Facebook and other social platforms based on our likes and dislikes.

I think what's going to be really exciting is when AI gets so commonplace that even shapes, structures, colours, typography, layout, and interactions are custom-created and optimised for your brain by artificial intelligence algorithms. That means we will all be able to learn and interact in a way that suits us.

A Totally New Trend is Coming

AI-powered design is on its way. There is already a new AI platform with the talent cutely named Molly. Molly is hosted by The Grid, where websites design themselves! Molly designs your content for you and claims that 'looking back three months from now she will have searched through more design decisions than stars in our galaxy'. That's impressive; and it's here already.

Take the idea a step further than website design and just imagine the implications. What if you could use an app for designing something you need – a piece of furniture, a car, even a new house? Imagine you can access the knowledge and processes of the best experts as if they were right next to you! All because AI technology had been able to map their judgement and decision processes and put them into a self-learning app. AI systems like these would have the potential to remember all the things you said and your instructions from all previous conversations, so these systems can make more and more decisions FOR you, and that will automate more and more processes in your life without actually programming it. It's a perfect parallel to the development of learning and embedding useful behaviour in the natural world.

Just think for a moment how much that could help you to amplify all your abilities and creativity. What could you do? The possibilities are infinite. That level of access to expertise to help discover the talents and gifts latent in everyone would expose genius that would have lain dormant. The world would be a very different place and the exponential growth of a more connected society would be assured.

Self-Programming Systems

Today, most of us have (or can remember) a family member, best friend, or partner who knows exactly how and when you like your breakfast and your coffee – not because you programmed it that way but because they learn from previous conversations and experiences and adapted their behaviour to suit your preferences. I believe that this is what automation and programming in the future looks like, only it will be driven by AI and not just by our human interactions. Just tell the system how you like it and software routines are created to suit your needs. It will all happen behind the scenes, so you probably won't be aware of it, but it will be happening. Just in the same way that Google already knows your personal preferences and the way Facebook already knows what you like and serves you with the content that it knows you like. In the future, with all the devices in your life being connected in some way, the sensors inside them will be able to predict what your next move is, and will even be able to suggest how to make your life more productive, effective, and purposeful. Amazon does that already with your reading choices. It's actually not that much of a leap.

Because AI systems can learn really quickly you won't have to tell the machines things twice – now, if you have children you will probably be able to imagine how wonderful that would be! In a world run by AI that might not have enough behaviour to go on and gets it wrong from time to time, it will be able to gauge your reaction, and if you don't feed back as the system expects you to it will have the capacity to ask how to improve that action in the future. We have that currently in some of the voice recognition apps, but by 2030 I'm confident that machines, sensors, and AI technology will be able to read non-verbal reactions too.

Imagine a machine having the emotional intelligence to read your gestures and emotions, or detect a change of tonality in your voice. We already have sensors that can measure your heart rate, stress levels, and many other physiological indicators, so I believe it's the connections to those devices that in the future will help our AI to help us by being able to sense if it is doing the right thing for you.

With this level of simplicity, even a four-year-old child will be able to start to automate all kind of processes, simply by talking to these kinds of systems.

With the rapid improvements in processing power and where we are on the S-curve at the moment, we really are mirroring what happens with biological organisms, and I believe that many essential processes in our society will be automated by 2030. Although automated processes are happening unconsciously in our bodies, they keep us alive. What would we do if our cells forgot to tell our heart to beat? Our technology will be running so many of our processes in the future, our ability to power that technology is going to be a massive shift and produce the reliability we need for that level of dependence. When automation is very reliable, cheap, and reliably powered, it will become unstoppable and everything that can be automated will be automated.

I am highly optimistic that the ultimate outcome of all this automation will be that we will be able to reach the top of the Maslow pyramid. That's a place where people are mainly busy with social, creative, moral, and meaningful work.

A place filled with meaningful work, and not meaning-less jobs. Now, isn't that something worth working towards for all of us?

From Mice to Memes – The Next Wave is Building

So the conditions are ready once again for the next phase of progress.

Where have we got so far? Time for a quick recap.

Our ancestors survived Wave 1.0 and started to cooperate with each other. Progress tipped over into Wave 2.0 with some basic infrastructure for moving stuff around, and we had the building blocks in place and reached a tipping point where we had sufficiently big networks that we had a new problem – and Wave 3.0 was triggered. Then there was plenty of information moving around the system, but things weren't very sophisticated. It was like all the instruments in an orchestra were playing, but it sounded pretty bad because nobody was organising the musicians! Sure, the pre-conditions were there for a great concert but we still had some key ingredients missing.

At the top of Wave 3.0 we now have all the players, but no conductor. What happens now is that the new problem is caused by the sheer amount of information. It's like there are sheets and sheets of music but no one has decided which tune to play first, so everyone is playing beautifully – but they are playing different tunes and there is no sense of timing or co-ordination. So there's a desperate need for a new level of intelligence. Without that, life gets more and more complicated instead of more and more simple. During Wave 3.0 the conductor steps in and starts to bring all the separate activities of the musicians into harmony, and beautiful things happen. The music starts to go from noise to melody. Progress can then be made and we can move to Wave 4.0 and make some of the background things happen automatically so the focus can be on the virtuoso performer.

Wave 4.0 is so exciting because progress has now reached an exponential phase on the S-curve. Now the conductor steps in and can deliver way above simply creating harmony. Amazing things happen now and the rate of change can speed up all over again. With the melody playing you can now detect the beauty of the individual instruments and so the performance can be increasingly refined. It's a similar process to what's in play when processing power doubles on a regular basis.

The constant doubling effect really starts to accelerate things. (Despite this, we are nowhere near physical limits yet. There is still plenty of room for improvement – and that means more disruption – and more opportunity.)

Yet again, the success of one layer creates a new problem that is the tipping point where the next layer becomes inevitable. As you know already, information won't be trapped, so progress **must** happen.

A problem created simply needs to be solved.

For the conductor to deliver a world-class performance from the orchestra, there's another ingredient that must go into the mix. An ingredient which if it's not there will be the start of discord. An orchestra is a great metaphor for a wider collective intelligence (and this exists in all great structures and communities from the smallest group of managers to the largest and most complex institutions). When there is collective intelligence there is significantly more room for error and, conversely, the greatest opportunities for creativity and change.

So to manage any level of collective intelligence, another ingredient is needed. An ingredient that goes beyond just routing data around.

You need **social connection**.

That's a Wave 5.0 solution. It's where magic happens. It's where new ideas and new developments start forming because information is flowing more freely and collaboration really starts to step up the rate of change. It happens in the animal kingdom, in Nature, inside communities of people, and it happens with technology too.

You could call what's coming next Wave 5.0 – the social wave. Wave 5.0 doesn't just hold the key to automation of more and more things; it also increases our social connections. We have seen exactly this playing out recently with the explosion of social media platforms.

The massive growth of platforms like Facebook, Twitter, Snapchat, and many others seemed to take people by surprise, but if they had been looking at the world with their Humanification glasses on, it would have been obvious that it was an inevitable development. Nature showed us the way. After things get more complex, when there are more patterns to manage and re-simplification has to happen, solutions that can undo the tangle soon emerge. And that leads neatly on to what has to happen in Wave 5.0. That's the further development and future of social sharing ... that's going to be the thing that untangles the spaghetti.

Chapter 31

Wave 5.0 – The Future is Social Sharing

Hardwired Intelligence

Human beings need to think. It's hardwired into us. Have you ever tried not to think about something? I could bet you $1,000 on the fact you have, and still ended up with your thoughts swirling over something.

How about when you have a brilliant insight or idea that could change things? Do you want to share it with someone while it's still fresh? Do you get a pang of disappointment if there is no one to bounce the idea around with?

There are two important forces at play here. They are twin forces that have sped up our development as human beings and have had a massive impact on where our technology has taken us in the last few years.

One force is the way our brain is wired to stay busy and the other is our need to connect with others. They are both old survival instincts that are still very much in evidence, but with a lack of sabre-toothed tigers, these days our behaviours play out differently.

You probably already know that it's almost impossible to quieten the mind, unless you seek and learn some strategies for deliberate intervention like meditation to 'turn your head off'. Even then, you have to think about it first and make a decision to do it! The alternative is to let our creative side run riot, self-medicate, or do one of the other key behaviours that we are strongly programmed to do: socialise with others. By socialising, we meet some of our deepest human needs. Maslow talked about our desire for belonging and love being one of our core human needs.

Thanks to Nature, our capacity for social activity is so sophisticated – largely because we have the brainpower for it. We have so many neural synapses and we need to give them something to do, and one of the ways we are hardwired to do our thinking is by collaborating with each other. Although it takes a lot of brainpower to do that, it also pools and leverages our collective brainpower. As a species, we achieve a great deal more as a community of minds than we could ever achieve in isolation. That's what Wave 5.0 is all about.

The Power of Collective Intelligence

This is the point in the wave cycle when we start operating together. It is just like a community of cells that are all working to help the whole community to go beyond mere survival. Nature follows the same patterns with groups of people too. There is a higher design that has already shown us that by working together we can thrive and create incredible things.

I often refer to Wave 5.0 as the social wave. In this wave, we can go beyond the needs of automating processes and heightening our senses and survival; we start to serve our cognitive and social needs.

The exciting thing about Wave 5.0 is that it also gives us a great deal of insight into how we ended up where we are. The more you understand about it, the more you get to see how the patterns of nature are repeated everywhere in our world. They're repeated in our relationships, our evolution, and our technology. Wave 5.0 doesn't just help us to predict what's coming; it also allows us to gain a much deeper understanding of where we are now and see the parallels with the past. And whenever we can draw parallels with the past, we get a glimpse of the solutions of the future.

Grow, Adapt, or Die

In the natural world, things are either growing, expanding, or they are dying. It seems that our intelligence and even our companies follow the same pattern. What is interesting is the patterns of the growth, because by connecting the patterns – and what's happened in natural history – that tells us a great deal about the next trends in both business and technology. And as you have already worked out, those two things have a closer link to each other now than at any other time in history.

Our cells are built to reproduce. Bigger groups of cells grow bigger structures, and so do people and communities. Small communities grow into villages, villages grow into towns, and towns grow into cities. In previous generations, all this happened fairly slowly, but with the increase in technology, transport, logistics and communications things are moving faster than ever before. But there is a limit on size. There comes a point when growing any bigger starts to cause more problems than it solves.

Our challenge as a society is coping with the transition between the size, scale, and solidity of our big companies and governments (and the benefits all those things brought) to a new economy. This new economy has to deal with the painful reality of the fact that a small number of big entities can no longer provide for us, simply because they were too slow to adapt to the changes that the internet and other fast-moving technologies brought to our world. They weren't lean, so they lagged, just as we had grown dependent on them.

We need to find new solutions to the challenge of growth, and it's my view that we can't solve these challenges alone. The exponential growth we have experienced in the last few generations can only be managed if we move to a society where we work together to solve our problems. But how did we get to this point? And what do Nature's patterns suggest to us about what is around the corner?

When Dinosaur Companies Ruled the World

In January 1905, thirty-six packing cases containing a very precious cargo indeed arrived at a London museum. They would go on to cause quite a stir. In the boxes were casts of bones found in Wyoming, USA, when a railway was being laid, and these were billed at the time as belonging to the 'Most Colossal Animal Ever on Earth'. The bones were owned by the nineteenth century industrialist and railway tycoon Andrew Carnegie. So popular was the idea of a massive animal that lived around 150 million years ago that Carnegie had casts made of the bones so that sets of bones could be gifted to favoured institutions around the world. He gifted a full set of casts of the Diplodocus bones to the London Natural History Museum.

The replica bones of Diplodocus Carnegii were unveiled to the public on 12 May 1905, and wowed audiences. The skeleton became a centrepiece of the museum and over 100 years later, Dippy (as he came to be known) holds pride of place in the hearts of millions. He has even been known to go on tour!

But here's the thing about Dippy: he may be impressive, he may be big, but he's notoriously difficult to move. It's a dinosaur trait. Being difficult to shift is a trait that many of our institutions share. Dinosaurs and institutions mirror each other in so many ways. They grew to a size for a good reason – the need for something big and stable was there, and the conditions to get to a massive size were right at the time of growth. And size equals stability, doesn't it? Well, yes, until conditions change. When that happens, size becomes a problem instead of a solution.

For decades, the industrialised parts of the world created a level of stability for big chunks of the population. In fact, the whole industrial and commercial model that we educate our kids in preparation for was built on the assumptions of big companies, stable jobs, big governments and long-term security. But it's not working out like that, is it?

In the past, we could educate our kids to be ready for a job with a large organisation or inside our governments, safe in the knowledge that they had a job for life if they wanted it. Their needs would be taken care of and life would be stable and predictable, and when they had done their time, they would be able to retire comfortably, knowing that the wealth they had generated during their lifetime would be paid back throughout their retirement.

But it's not turning out that way. We are educating people for something that no longer exists. And yet if we look back to the dinosaurs, those big lumbering beasts that fascinate us so much, we can learn a lot about our organisations, the job market, how we need to educate the next generation and how things are going to progress. You may even spot multiple opportunities for new ways to do business too ...

So let's compare the (often struggling) dinosaur companies with the real ones that roamed around our planet years ago – a useful thing to do because they have more in common with what's going on now that you might first think.

It's easy to think of dinosaurs as a short-lived group of creatures, but in fact they were incredibly successful for millions of years. Our corporations haven't lasted that long, but there are common threads and by looking at some of the compatibles you can learn a great deal and use that knowledge to see where things are going inside your own industry. Are you in a progressive business? Are you educating yourself and your children in a way that will help them survive in the future? Are you geared up for success, or extinction?

The dinosaurs had a very stable life for a long time. They didn't have to do much other than eat and move around slowly. There was plenty of space on the planet so there wasn't a great deal of competition for food, so they could eat all they wanted. That's why they were able to grow so big. Their only limits were the physical limits of gravity, bone density, and the need to move around to escape threats or chomp on the next tree.

For millions of years the earth was a pretty stable place for them to develop. Their size will have made it hard to move quickly because it would have taken massive amounts of energy to do that. It's like that for many of the long-established big companies of today. Fast movement and sudden adaptation isn't easy when you reach a large size. Change was slow, adaptation could take as long as it needed to, and things weren't all that difficult. All that's fine until something hits out of the blue – like a meteor (or the internet).

Meteor Alert!

Then, out of the blue, in one day, everything changed. It probably could be seen from a long way away. Only the most agile got out of the way in time to survive. Some of the smaller ones far away from the epicentre found shelter because they were able to move quickly and find shelter; they adapted quickly (and were the ancestors to our modern birds).

That was around 66 million years ago, but the lessons still stand. Get too big, get too complacent, and something will eventually explode or come out of the blue and there won't be time to react and survive.

For the last couple of centuries, our world has been dominated by wealthy power bases of some description, either multinational corporations, large power-based families, or religious institutions. All of these have dinosaur characteristics: they are slow to adapt and change, too big to move quickly, and have gotten used to getting their energy from a reliable and easy-to-access source, rather like their prehistoric counterparts! For the sake of shorthand, let's refer to the group as multinationals for now.

It makes perfect economic sense why they behaved the way they did, and how they came to get big and slow. Life was reliable and slow, and they only used valuable energy when things got tough. Moving quickly gets tough when you are so big.

The multinationals' meteor came from cyberspace. And, like all things sudden, its rise was exponential and they just didn't see it coming. Within a few short years, advertising changed, you didn't need a massive film crew to create an advert anymore; you only needed an HD smartphone. You didn't need a big advertising agency to come up with creative ideas; you could have an idea and then film it and get it on TV or a platform like YouTube or Vimeo in a matter of hours. Smaller businesses could adapt and evolve, but the dinosaurs struggled to change fast enough. In the gap that was left, small companies came up with new ideas faster than the dinosaur companies thought possible.

Now, we are all linked through our smartphones. We all have access to suppliers from all over the world. Today almost anyone can produce a product, think of a transformational idea and get it funded, develop an app, and reach a market on the other side of the planet. Dinosaurs can do so too – they still have a level of power and wealth – but things have changed so fast that they dinosaurs can't keep up and many of them live in fear. There are some massive companies who don't fit into the dinosaur category, but if you look at them more closely you suddenly realise that their size hides their history. These companies (like Apple, Microsoft, Google, and Amazon) started small, grew quickly, and were themselves based on disruptive ideas and technologies. They might be big, but they place high value on innovation, flexibility, and creative thinking.

The Biggest Wave of All

Almost everyone can still recall the horrific images of the tsunami when it hit the coast of Phuket in Thailand back in 2004.

One minute, people were standing on glorious white sand beaches. Then a few moments later there were videos taken as the water pulled so far back that coral reefs along the coast were laid bare and began to dry.

Tourists and residents were bemused. They didn't know what was coming. In the distance, a thin white line appeared on the horizon. It rapidly got closer. For a few short minutes and seconds, people didn't know what they were seeing. They stood on the shoreline in wonder. But as the line approached, the people near the water's edge realised with horror that it wasn't a mysterious illusion – it was a huge tidal wave of roaring white water, and it was going to wipe out the ground they stood on.

It was too late to flee. As the wave hit, the first boats capsized and were smashed to pieces. The tsunami hit the coast with devastating force. It dragged everything in its path with it. The result was disastrous; the entire coastline was swept underwater.

In total, authorities estimated that more than 230,000 people were killed that day, over fourteen countries. There were over a million casualties.

Livelihoods were destroyed, families torn apart, and entire communities laid to waste.

Technology has done the same in some places on our planet and in some industries. But that has always been the case; it's not a new phenomenon. Technology, from the printing press to the railways, has a long history of wiping out entire industries. But all new developments have created a wealth of opportunities too. That's more than can be said for the natural tragedy that happened over the 2004 festive holiday.

The impact of the internet on the economy has caused a tsunami of technological developments coming at us at high speed. Just like the sea withdrew in Phuket, we now see a retreating movement of consumers (and workers) from the more traditional organisational structures. More and more people are turning away from the large, impersonal chain stores and order their products online and stay at home to consume them.

This time it's not the coral reefs along the coast that are dry, but it is the large concrete buildings of bankrupt chain stores that have been too big to keep up with trends and too slow to see the internet boom and the change in our shopping habits.

Never before has confidence in sectors such as government, healthcare, and financial systems been as low as now. The water level is being kept artificially high. In reality, the coral reefs are dry and most people are trying not to notice. The water level has dropped below viable levels, but currently there is still an attempt being made to keep going as if everything was okay.

It's not okay. And you need to be prepared. You need to be ready to adapt. You need to stay agile and be able to anticipate future events. You need to expect the unexpected and be ready to spot things coming over the horizon before they wipe you out.

If you are running or working for a traditional, linear, and inflexible organisation then it might be a good idea to look out to sea and watch for the signs. The future is in sharing ideas, collaboration with other people, and seeing opportunities by connecting with others. Our governments and institutions are not going to be able to look after us in the same way our parents expected them to. You are going to have to link with other people to make the positive changes you want to see in the world.

Lessons From the Arab Spring: The Surprising Uprising

On 17 September 2010, in Ben Arous, north-east Tunisia, a street vendor named Tarek al-Tayeb Mohamed Bouazizi decided he'd had enough of the bullying that had blighted his little business. He'd had enough of the alleged corrupt municipal enforcement officials who had moved him on and confiscated his goods once too often.

Bouazizi's response was to set himself on fire.

His story added fuel to an already burning cauldron of resentment inside Tunisia and set off what became the Tunisian Revolution, part of the wider Arab Spring movement. In previous decades, Bouazizi's death would have been a locally reported incident in a place where mainstream media was tightly controlled. But things had changed: the smartphone, social media, and digital technology suddenly allowed citizens to communicate and tell their stories outside the traditional broadcasting channels.

What's fascinating is that, according to Amnesty International and other research bodies, social media (in particular Twitter, Facebook, and other local social platforms) played a key role in toppling governments relatively peacefully. Citizens were able to communicate, connect, and mobilise large groups outside the traditional communications channels. It gave political activism a huge boost that the authorities had never experienced before. During the Arab Spring, people even created pages on Facebook to raise awareness about alleged crimes against humanity, such as the police brutality in the Egyptian Revolution. It's getting harder and harder for regimes to keep secrets as there is a watching public on almost every street corner. Increasingly, people have a smartphone to record what they see, and an internet connection to publish across the globe within seconds.

Beyond Information Sharing

Increasingly we aren't just sharing information; the growing trend is that we are starting to share our assets as well. Since the development of more and more platforms that allow us to share specific things, sharing our assets has gone virtual – and viral. Look how far we have come in just a few short years:

- We share use of our homes on Airbnb, Flipkey or HomeAway
- We share use of our vehicles with Uber, Blabla, Lyft, or Turo

- We share our trust by accepting payments in virtual currencies like bitcoin
- We share our offices and meeting spaces on LiquidSpace and all-desk
- We share our experiences, using mixed and virtual reality.

So what's next for the future of social sharing? Let's step into the future for a moment and see what life might look like in 2030 . . .

Imagine the Power of Human Collective Intelligence

Just for a moment, imagine your favourite football team (if you aren't a football fan, feel free to substitute a music artist) performing before an audience of 20,000+ people. Now imagine you are one of the people in that audience.

The moment is building. That moment when the football player has just scored that important goal (or your favourite artist is playing that #1 song) and the entire audience explodes and moves in the same rhythm. At that very moment the audience becomes as one; a harmonious and coherent community behaving as one single organism. At that exact moment, incredible amounts of energy are released. As one of the audience, you can feel it. You are a part of it. You are it. It's powerful stuff.

What happens when an entire country celebrates winning like that? Now, instead of a crowd of 20,000 or 30,000 people, imagine a crowd of hundreds of millions of people, or even a billion highly connected people. What happens when that many souls start to act like one single organism and achieve one very hard-to-reach goal?

Now, with that euphoric crowd in mind, imagine what that highly connected group of people will be able to do when they join forces? Billions of bright minds are now online and connected and they all share their ideas, emotions, thoughts, and feelings. Innovation has exploded; every individual now has the power to create and launch new innovative products and services and make a big impact within their own community. There is almost no problem left that can't be solved by smart online social communities empowered by advanced software and unlimited machine learning power in the cloud.

That's Humanification. That's the future we are heading for. That's something worth having.

Chapter 32

Wave 5.0 – Sharing Trends

So what are we likely to be sharing very soon? Here are some of the up-and-coming technologies that are probably going to be making an appearance in your life before very long.

Sharing your Experiences

At the time of writing there's a working prototype of a pair of polarised glasses that allow you to record your 360-degree experiences exactly as you see them, with all the technology built directly into a pair of normal-looking sunglasses. In essence, the device – called ORBI Prime – is four water-resistant, high-resolution cameras that record the world just like you see it. Then there's Insta360, a little device that attaches to your smartphone and allows you to turn your phone into a smart 360-degree virtual reality camera. Devices like this are going to change the way we share out experiences forever. You can already buy virtual reality headsets with data beamed back from a drone, so although you might not be able to fly like Superman round the Grand Canyon, you can feel like you are by attaching a camera and beaming it back to immersive experience goggles (subject to local laws, which are tightening by the day for understandable safety reasons).

Then there's seventies sci-fi coming to life with hologram calls, where you can trick your brain into feeling like you are sharing the same space with the person at the other end of the call. Microsoft have been showcasing this technology that captures high-quality 3D images and displays them back to the wearer of their mixed reality display glasses, the HoloLens. Recently they have even been able to compress the data to a point where they did a demo, projecting the image to a vehicle, taking the experience out of the lab and into the real world for the first time.[25]

---

[25] https://www.microsoft.com/en-us/research/project/holoportation-3/

And what if you could wear a virtual reality mask that could record your facial expressions and imprint those on to a virtual avatar of you in real time? Well, it's more than close; it's here already. Veeso, a virtual reality (VR) start-up, have produced a VR headset with built-in face-tracking cameras and infrared sensors that track your eyes, mouth, and jawline and then bluetooths the data out to your virtual avatar. It's a leap forward in sharing your emotions using virtual technology.

What about a car that you could steer with your mind? Mind-controlled movement is something that scientists have been working on for a long time but we are getting closer all the time. Back in 2014 on a disused airfield, Henrik Matzke drove a car with his brainpower alone. It was part of a project called BrainDriver,[26] which is aiming to help people to use brainpower for all sorts of applications. The hope is that it won't just be cars we could control by thought alone, but wheelchairs and prosthetic limbs too.

If the future is going to be all about sharing, what about sharing our ideas and having them listened to and peer-reviewed? Up until recently, despite readily available internet access, scientific discoveries have still depended on publication in a major journal before they are taken seriously. That affects research budgets and even skews how research is presented. A new platform called *ScienceMatters*[27] is providing a democratised platform in an attempt to get smaller ideas exposed to peer review faster so that these potentially valuable seed ideas can be built on faster than has traditionally been possible.

It's likely that there are going to be more and more opportunities for people without an Ivy-League-style academic background to be recognised for their ideas, and that is going to be yet another factor that will accelerate technology's progress faster than has been possible before.

Sharing Trust

We have talked about blockchain a lot already because it's a key technology that's going to impact all of our lives sooner or later. It's highly relevant to Wave 5.0 developments due to the sharing element, because the whole principle allows for secure transactions. Recently, two of the Middle East's

---

[26] http://www.bbc.com/future/story/20140620-i-drove-a-car-with-my-thoughts
[27] www.sciencematters.io

biggest banks have partnered on a blockchain project. Dubai's largest bank, Emirates NBD, and India's ICICI Bank launched a blockchain network and are already using it to make transactions. What would have previously taken days of authentication, processing, and delivery have been completed in just minutes.

So where is all this sharing technology going to take us?

The Wave 5.0 Social DNA Trend

I believe that in the future the core of every new initiative is going to be social. It's in the DNA of everything we do now. Billions of new people are now connected through the internet and the number of people coming online is still increasing every day. The web is going to become the nervous system of the human race. If humanity were a car (and we are certainly an engine that drives things forward) then over time, as we add people to the web, it's like adding extra cylinders to the engine of your car. With every extra cylinder, the car has more power and torque and it can go faster and faster. For the first time since the dawn of humanity, the engine of our society has the potential to run on full power. When the entire world population is connected then all the cylinders are going to be firing at the same time. I'm incredibly optimistic that our increased social accountability and our desire to connect with each other on a local level will see the greatest increase in our happiness over the next few decades. It certainly has the potential for that, once we get used to the fact we can't slow down the pace of change.

I refer to the new era that's on the way as 'The WE society' or the 'WEconomy' (as opposed to the ME society), and I believe it's one of the biggest goals we can achieve as humanity.

The WEconomy is a social and coherent society of highly connected people that work together as one organism. In the future, if we manage it well, I believe we have the potential to act as if we were one highly intelligent organism that treats itself (and the earth we live on) with the care and respect it deserves. Humanity has a bright future, and you are part of it. We are all part of it; starting today.

Chapter 33

Living in a Wave 5.0 World

A Day in the Future of Sharing

I predict that when we wake up in 2030 we will probably see that social sharing has reached its mature phase. We already share our very intimate things like thoughts with other people all over the world (though how we edit them for sharing can be a challenge).

In the last two decades, we learned that the more we shared, the more we received in return.

Virtual Reality Comes of Age

It is now possible to share fully immersive experiences that involve almost all of your senses. You can record your experiences with a head-mounted communication device in ultra-high resolution. What you see and hear and smell is an experience that can be recorded and shared in the way that people shared videos on YouTube in the early twenty-first century. People can 'live' your experiences as if they were their own, and you can 'live' theirs too. As so many of your senses are involved, your brain believes you are actually experiencing these VR recordings and it's given all of us a whole new perspective on life. You can now experience almost everything you can imagine. If someone has experienced it first-hand and shared it online, you can too.

Live broadcasting has also improved. You can also real-time share your presence or experience with other people, like a live broadcast. It started with live streaming on social platforms a few years ago and has grown from there. Just imagine being able to experience what a #1 football player is experiencing during a World Cup match, living the experience real-time and live in the moment! Livestreams have even more impact than recordings because someone else is experiencing it at the same moment. In fact, there can be millions of people who can have exactly the same experience at the same time.

In the same way that a crowd in a sports stadium feels the atmosphere and the power of a group, VR will be able to do the same thing and make these shared experiences more powerful and emotional. Want to live the life of a rock star? Maybe you want to test out the life of an athlete or a movie star? Then tune in and test it out! Shared experiences and being 'virtually present' is so enjoyable; as well as being great entertainment, it's easy to forget just what a powerful learning tool it is.

Just think of how this shared experience gives us the chance to eliminate negative experiences too. Imagine if we could experience the lives, experiences, and interactions of other people who have a more difficult life than we do. Things could be so different. Imagine what it would be like to be in a minority, a misunderstood group, or maybe you are being bullied or pushed around? Then you suddenly have the chance to share what it's like to live your life. You could allow people to see life from a different point of view. It could change everything.

Imagine the power that true experience-sharing could have on our skills and abilities to model and learn from the best of the best. With this technology you can tune in to the best person in the field and really see and feel how they do what they do. If you want to learn something new, all you have to do is tune into the experience or presence of someone that is the very best in this specific arena.

With 2030 VR technology, so many of your senses are involved, your brain is much more active and involved. That means you can learn much faster than just reading about it or watching a video. You can actually live it because your brain is tricked into thinking that your own body is doing it already. Your neural networks in your brain light up like crazy and start to build the deep-imprinted patterns of learning. Having experienced the neural patterns of a top football player/musician/skier/tennis pro, your brain is already wired to start building new connections. You have had the experience for the first time the right way. Of course, you still need to practise because you need to condition your body, but you will have a massive advantage.

Become a Machine

Just imagine if you could go one step further. What if you could also not just tune into people's experiences, but also tune into the experiences of a robot? It's not that far-fetched. You can already tune into the senses of a drone flying across the Grand Canyon. What if you could become the rocket that goes on tour to the moon? Or you could tune into a walking robot and visit a remote or dangerous place on earth, travel under the sea, explore the deep abyss in the Atlantic ocean, or swim with the fish on a coral reef?

Share Your Brainwaves!

In 2035 our head-mounted communication devices are so small we can wear them all the time without noticing them. These nano-computers are so sophisticated they can detect and record your most subtle brainwaves and thought patterns. If you can detect things and record them, they can be transmitted to someone else by being projected on the brains of the person who wants to understand, share, or learn.

We have actually got to the point where computing and communications technology allows us to transmit thoughts, emotions and feelings to other people.

What about receiving thoughts from other people? Well, your head-mounted communication device receives signals from someone else, decodes it to your brain preferences, and stimulates specific parts of your brain with weak electromagnetic fields and patterns that simulate certain thoughts, feelings, and emotions. You no longer have to feel the way you do if you don't want to. If you are feeling sad you can tune into happy feelings on your device, which your device will have learned from a time when you were happy or tuned into a happy person. (Sound far-fetched? There is already a company that does that: Thync[28] is a wearable technology that gently stimulates nerves on the head and neck with safe, low-level electrical pulses that make you feel better, and was developed by a team of neuroscientists from MIT, Harvard, and Stanford.)

Although every brain is programmed and mapped slightly differently, advanced machine learning algorithms can now read and map patterns from one brain and transfer them to another brain. It is even possible to transform patterns from one brain template to the other in real time.

---

[28] http://www.thync.com

Your thoughts can trigger certain emotions and feelings. That has always been true for us, but now we can transfer emotions and feelings to other people by transferring thoughts to them. There is incredible power to being able to do this. So much of top performance is about a state that scientists often refer to as 'flow', and this technology allows us to share a 'flow' state with others. That allows us to learn new skills faster than before. It goes way beyond simply sharing video, because flow stimulates more neural networks in your brain. Kids could learn to play a guitar without ever reading one musical note and get the feeling of total focus and relaxation at the same time. More flow means better music, and better music increases flow. Everyone wins when we can share positive emotion and link that to performance. People can now know what if feels like to succeed.

Our ability to transfer knowledge and insights from one human to another has profoundly changed how we improve the quality of our lives.

Knowledge WAS Power, Now Sharing IS Power

In 2030 we live in a world where knowledge is democratised. In other words, knowledge is now accessible for everybody. Over the past couple of decades it seems that free access to knowledge was the best tool we had. It helped us to solve many of the world's greatest and most mysterious questions. Greater access by a larger number of powerful thinkers led to more knowledge and became a wonderful ingredient to boost scientific discoveries and breakthroughs.

We now have technology platforms that gather, validate, and share scientific knowledge with the community. Remember that the internet started to gather fans in the early days through the universities, so it has always been the fields of science and research that have led the way in the field of sharing; they still do. It's now more than a decade since the scientific world was first disrupted when the traditional peer-reviewed science became free for everyone to review on a large scale. This was the point when anyone who was interested was able to become a scientist. If you wanted to submit observations and research results on the big review platforms, all you needed was a genuine interest and a computer connection. The elite status dropped away and we could all get involved. You no longer had to have the time, money, or connections to mix with the top people in any one field. You could be part of the review process or even the science itself. We have even moved on since then. Now, in 2030, advanced machine learning algorithms are used to validate, cross-check, and connect all newly added knowledge. Our learning machines can create one single version of the truth that is accessible for everyone for free. Everybody can tap into this huge database of validated and cross-linked knowledge. It makes the old-style 'Wikipedia', the first widely used knowledge platform, look like kindergarten! (Though it's still going and continues to be a popular knowledge-sharing platform today.)

It's not just the scientific communities that share these days. Public organisations, communities, and commercial entities have to publish all their knowledge to these platforms. In the early twenty-first century, the process of obtaining information was there, but it was laborious and had to be conducted through a long-winded Freedom of Information process. Now, there is much more available in the public domain and we are all better off for it because accountability breeds trust. And trust is a commodity that helps us all.

The Death of the Middleman and The Rise of Trust

Today, in 2030, every digital identity, law, vote, contract, regulation, currency, media, or other valuable piece of data is stored and tracked by a decentralised, encrypted, and secure network of computers owned by all of us. So what runs the network and how does it work? Well, the network is essentially a chain of computers and every single one of them must approve an exchange of data before it can be verified and recorded. We call this decentralised and encrypted and secure database the 'Digital Ledger', and it totally eliminates the need for a middleman, or trusted third party. Why do you need a trusted advisor when the data itself is trustworthy? In 2030, everybody can do trusted transactions, and everyone on the network can see what the audit trail is. You don't need a middleman any more and the entire system employs a high level of cryptography to keep all our exchanges secure. Back in the early twenty-first century the idea was referred to as the blockchain. It was the starting point for our modern Digital Ledger. Things are cheaper because we don't need an introducer anymore; we can all deal direct. The middleman businesses started to disappear a few years ago as the 20% and 30% margins on a transaction that couldn't go wrong became outdated. The earlier twentieth century disruptors of their time like Google, Amazon, and Apple had to change radically to survive when the margin model was circumvented by clever users who were all connected. Add to that the fact that we suddenly no longer needed the insurance that these old-style middle men provided. It was built into the transaction. Products and services got cheaper, the sellers got more value, and the buyer got a cheaper product.

It caused a huge disruption around 2020, but things soon settled down as middlemen and brokers started to come up with new ways of adding value rather than adding margin.

The first large-scale implementation of this distributed trust system (somewhere around 2020) had big implications for our monetary system and the traditional institutes that had their foundations in the old system. They had been crumbling for a long time, and eventually the debt-laden institutions couldn't cope when people regained ownership of their money. Virtual currencies became the norm and people took direct control over their preferred medium of exchange, leaving the traditional institutes like banks, central banks, and governments floundering. It was a breath of fresh air (despite the massive uncertainty at the time). When the changes took hold, the new system made shady markets transparent again and virtual identities and products trustworthy. In 2030 you can sell products or services to anyone in the world and you know you are going to get a fair price and that your buyer is someone trustworthy. They can't defraud the system, and blockchain keeps everyone protected.

Shared Transport and Logistics

Nowadays, not many of us own cars anymore; we share them with other people instead. It's hard to imagine that there was a time when we had a car on nearly every driveway and we spent so much time travelling alone. But although most things have gone virtual, the things we do have are shared in a very efficient way. Advanced technology makes it possible for us to all share assets, and it's not even a hassle.

Need a car or transport? Then in 2030 you simply ask for it and it usually arrives within minutes (or even seconds on a good day!). There's no need to have valuable assets like cars that you only use for an hour or two out of twenty-four. It's so much better that you only use what you need when you need it. In between, things return to the shared pool. We all travel lighter, don't carry so much around with us, and are much more mobile than we used to be. Our transport systems work in a much more natural way and our modern systems were modelled on our blood cells (people) and veins and arteries in our bodies (our rail/roads/networks). Think about it: our bodies are incredibly efficient. Even the tiny space inside our red blood cells is not wasted. When we realised that in healthy conditions more than 95% of the oxygen capacity in our cells is utilised, we started to ask questions about the spare space in our cars and other transport systems. We learned from our blood, which is amazing stuff. The reason blood is so incredibly efficient is that our red blood cells aren't dedicated to specific organs or tissues. If they were, we would probably have traffic jams in our veins. Our blood cells are shared by all the organs of our body. We have a massive network inside our bodies. It's like a giant transport and logistics lab, and sometime early in the century we started to realise we could model our own physical efficiency in the world around us. Our personal internal network is so extensive, each one of our 10 trillion cells gets its own deliveries of oxygen precisely when it needs them. Blood is both a collective and individual form of transportation. Just amazing. So next time you cut yourself, instead of just wiping away the red stuff, take a moment to marvel at it.

Biology, and even slime mould, is very efficient. Following on from innovative work of the Japanese back in the twentieth century using slime mould to design the most efficient routes, using Nature to help us plan has become commonplace.

Back in the twentieth century, most of our transport networks were two-dimensional. More recently we have worked out that we have much more space to work with than we had with our old-paradigm thinking.

Our modern shared transport system is now a 3D transportation network, more like the network of veins in your body. With our roads now occupied mainly by autonomous vehicles, and our airspace busy with autonomous flying drones that transport people and goods, we now think in cubic space rather than in square metre space. Our infrastructure is now a quantum leap more efficient that it was in the days of fossil-fuel-powered vehicles. The challenge of traffic management has dissolved now that artificial intelligence is controlling the fleets and complexities because it sees the whole thing as one single system, just like the blood cells in our veins sees the body as one system.

Sharing Will Become the New Normal

Although this imaginary tour through our shared future is a construct of my lively imagination (though, as you know, based on patterns that exist already, and not just on some mad cap visions), it has profound implications.

Sharing information about unfair treatment has the power to make the world a profoundly fairer place. Sharing a secure medium of exchange is going to challenge governments and is going to change how we raise taxes and pay for shared infrastructure. The idea of a digital ledger is going to change commerce and the role of brokers and middlemen, and the potential for sharing our experience and feelings with others has the capacity to change how we treat our fellow man. As we move further and further towards a shared society based on trust, we are going to have some big challenges to deal with. We are going to need to create new support structures, new ways of doing business, new ways of looking after people in society who can't look after themselves and many other ways of taking care of our planet. It won't be an easy ride all the way – disruption caused by new technology never gives us that – but it does give us opportunities greater than most of us can possibly imagine. What I can promise to you is that you will have more information at your fingertips in the next five years than has ever been available to humanity before, and the better the interfaces get with the tech in your everyday life, the more you will use it and the richer your life will become. So the next question has to be: what is the future of learning? What form will it take? And how will that affect us, our kids, and the people who are going to be looking after us when we get older? Let's find out.

Chapter 34

Wave 6.0 –
The Future of Learning

The Rumble in the Concrete Jungle

The complex and subtle game of Go originated in China over 2,500 years ago. It's essentially a simple game. Players take turns to place black or white stones on a board. The simple objectives are to gain territory by either capturing the opponent's stones or surrounding empty space so you own the territory.

The rules may be very simple but Go is a game of profound complexity. Even though the board is only nineteen lines across and nineteen lines down, there are more possible positions than there are atoms in the known universe. That makes Go a googol times more complex than the game of chess (If you haven't used a googol lately, it's a 1 followed by a hundred zeros; that's a very big number ...). So you can understand how it is that Go has a level of complexity that has confounded computers.

As with all fascinating challenges, where there's a metaphorical mountain to climb, there are people who want to climb it. The Go challenge was no different. There is a team of dedicated people obsessed with solving the puzzle of getting a computer to beat a human at Go. So, in March 2016 the stage was set and the challenge was on.

A new programme called AlphaGo had been developed by a crack team of experts at Google DeepMind, Google's artificial intelligence unit in London, and it was ready to be unleashed. The event was to be a game where AlphaGo, the machine, met its human counterpart. The AI programme was booked to play the legendary Go player Lee Sedol from South Korea. Sedol had been the top Go player in the world over the past decade. It was a best-of-five match.

It was a much-anticipated match. The match was booked to take place at the Four Seasons Hotel, Seoul, South Korea, on 9, 10, 12, 13 and 15 March. It was to be livestreamed from the stylish skyscraper on DeepMind's own YouTube channel, and there was intense media interest and so traditional media was broadcasting it on TV throughout Asia.

The fans of Go, from Korea, China, Japan, and all over the world, watched intently. Surely no computer could beat a player at Go, could it? Go is a subtle game that's played primarily through intuition and feel, and because of its beauty, subtlety, and intellectual depth it has captured the human imagination for centuries. So there was a great deal at stake. Could it be done? Had AI and machine learning come far enough to challenge the world's best player?

To the surprise of many, the computer won 4–1. It was, literally, a game-changing match. AlphaGo was the first computer program to ever beat a professional human player. AlphaGo used a new level of machine learning to master the ancient game and it showed definitively that computing was on the exponential part of the S-curve.

The big technology companies aren't just employing programmers; they also attract the best minds in fields from engineering to neuroscience – people who are passionate about understanding our world and how technology can be used to make it better. The brightest minds of our day are collaborating on making technology more human, more useable, and more available to us all. In my opinion, the future is very bright indeed if you are nimble, curious, and adaptable – in other words, the opposite of a dinosaur.

From Data to Intelligence

The Data Revolution

The automation and social wave produced tons and tons of data. There is data about our interactions between us and our technology, there are data records of our communication amongst ourselves – our digital communication footprint. There is financial data, experience data, and data about our finances, energy, and a thousand other things. In other words, there is more data than we humans can possibly digest. So that means we are going to constantly need new technology that can glean useful things from all the information we generate in earlier waves. But there is another level of data management, and that using data to truly learn; that's in contrast to data that is stored as a fixed conscious memory. And there is a big difference.

In October 2016, my son Ruben came into the world. From the moment he arrived, he was 'programmed' for survival. From day one, his brain knew how to take care of all his automated functions. His 'reptile' brain just knew that it had to look after his breathing. His 'automated systems' took care of his blood pressure, his digestive system, and body temperature. Ruben was programmed by instinct to keep his own body in a stable state; in homeostasis.

Within minutes, his social brain recognises the voice and smell of my wife and the all-important social bond starts building in strength and the resulting trust kicks in too. He instinctually knows that being with his mother is a safe place to be. As soon as he is able, he will be able to copy the movements, facial expressions, and behaviours of his mother, of me, and his siblings. It's a miracle of nature that both his reptilian brain and the social brain are pre-programmed and have worked almost entirely automatically from the very moment of his birth.

Ruben's neocortex, the outermost part of his brain – involved in his higher functions of sensory perception, generation of motor commands, his spatial reasoning, conscious thought, and his language – is an incredible flexible learning space and needs time to develop. Our brains are amazing things that develop from back to front. Directly after birth, Ruben's learning process will start the same way yours did: in a specific sequence. First, before he can start moving around, he's going to need to be able to process and understand what he's seeing, otherwise it won't be safe to move around. He will need to hear and process sound before he can develop speech.

Just like the 7 Waves of Innovation, one level of development is required before the next is possible. Each wave builds on the one that came before. One skill builds on the one that was developed before. Following the same principle, one level of intelligence can spring from the intelligence that came into existence because of an earlier learning 'experience'.

The machine learning revolution we are now entering is also following a specific development sequence, and because we know the patterns of the waves that nature illustrates so beautifully for us we can now predict that development sequence. We know that each wave needs the existence and maturity of the previous one to create the next. We are well into a phase of social sharing. It's nowhere near full maturing yet, with sharing platforms only really just starting to become mainstream. But with the pace of change picking up (because we are in an exponential growth phase), we know that the uptake of social sharing is moving so fast that it won't be long before the next wave starts to build up some power.

My prediction is that humanity is about to enter Wave 6.0 – the intelligence wave. Wave 5.0 saw the advent of a sharing explosion. Wave 6.0 is going to herald a new level of shared intelligence: artificial intelligence and machine learning.

From Information to Transformation

So, if we are in the process of moving from a Wave 5.0 (the sharing wave) to Wave 6.0 (the intelligence wave), the big question then becomes: what changes are we likely to experience?

As always, Nature is the ultimate inspiration. So let's use that as a kick-off point. We have talked a lot about the development of our neocortex. Just think for a moment about how that changed us. As we, as a species, developed a more and more sophisticated brain function we were able to learn faster and faster. We learned to use tools, to start fires, and we rapidly developed our language. Although scientists can't seem to agree when and how language started, there's no doubt it wouldn't have been possible without our massively increased brainpower. The more we could communicate and express our desires, the more we were able to see our dreams become reality. That resulted in art, architecture, and the great civilisations that contributed to our knowledge and our science.

Now take that level of shift, from primitive caveman to the sophistication of culturally rich, modern man, and imagine the potential for that level of learning to be condensed into a few short generations. It's difficult to comprehend just what the impact on humanity will be when we have a virtual neocortex located in the cloud. And yet, that's exactly what's happening. It gives a new meaning to the old expression 'head in the clouds'. Our collective virtual brain, with its massive storage capacity, algorithms that learn at lightning speed and greater flexibility and sharing potential than ever before, is going to herald a new world, the likes of which we have never even imagined.

Our future lies in our ability to use this power for preservation of the incredibly diverse plant life, animals, and habitats that we have the privilege to share our planet with. We have almost infinite capacity for change and learning. We have the power to use it for positive change. It's up to us. We have control. We have choice. We have the imagination.

It's in the power of our imagination that our future lies. So the ultimate question for our future can only be this: just how big can we dream?

Chapter 35
Wave 6.0 – Trends

Medical Revolutions

Back at the beginning of this book we talked about how it was time for the world to belong to the entrepreneurs. The time of the old dinosaur companies is passing and the new power is with the creators of technology. Well, one of the first companies to make it big in the data space of the technology industry is proving to be at the start of using its algorithm technology and expertise in big data to help medicine move to a new level.

Recently, Google published a paper in the *Journal of the American Medical Association* that gave details of a brand-new algorithm that is so sophisticated that it can detect when someone has developed blindness as a result of diabetes. The algorithm itself was trained and tested by board-certified ophthalmologists. Google have been able to demonstrate that it works as well as diagnosis by professional human ophthalmologists. That's probably because the algorithm itself was trained via a panel of certified ophthalmologists who hand-graded nearly 130,000 images, the data from which was used to teach the algorithm.

'I remain convinced that we have yet to see a machine outperform a doctor in any task that is relevant to actual medical practice,' qualified radiologist Oakden-Rayner recently wrote in a blog post. Sentences later, he continues, 'While I was writing this, literally this last paragraph, it became untrue.'

It's turning out that, rather than removing the human element to medicine, it's more likely that algorithms will give doctors more time to spend with their patients, and less time reading scans.

If you had said twenty years ago that a search engine company would be at the forefront of medical research, you would have probably been avoided in your local village. How times change. The growth of mini-learning machines like these algorithms is going to re-shape medicine. Unlike people, an algorithm is scalable, reliable, and cheap to deploy. They are also a virtual asset so don't need to be physically moved around. They are a dematerialised gift to medicine. The more medical imaging tasks they can take on, the greater the scope for good.

It's going to be a while before algorithms are making real diagnoses in hospitals, but it's getting closer every day. Google have announced already that they're talking to the Food and Drug Administration in the USA and other regulators on building trials. Things are moving really fast. Google's sister firm DeepMind is working closely with the UK's National Health Service retinal image analysis and are even looking at an AI application for cancer diagnosis and treatment. They are working in partnership with University College London on using AI to guide cancer treatments for head and neck cancers. The DeepMind researchers will get access to anonymous radiology scans from up to 700 former patients, so they can use them to teach algorithms to learn the visual difference between healthy and cancerous tissue.

There is also work going on with similar machine learning to diagnose breast cancer with ever-increasing accuracy and a reduced rate of 'false positives'. Samsung Medison, the South Korean tech company's medical device arm, recently developed a new ultrasound machine that uses deep learning to quickly spot if breast tissue is cancerous or benign. The machine's algorithm was trained on 9,000 real breast tissue scans.

Once again, the algorithms are learning from thousands of previous scans and previous outcomes, and treatment can be targeted with laser accuracy. Algorithms are being used to monitor patients with kidney disease. The applications that are possible are getting closer and closer to maturity that will allow for better and earlier diagnosis and give doctors more time to target confirmed disease. The medical facilities of your local doctor are likely to look very different in just ten years' time. And if you follow the curve of the natural development of miniaturisation that we talked about in the earlier waves, it's more and more likely that the wearable technology of the future will diagnose on the go and remove much of the need for manual diagnostics anyway. Now, wouldn't that be better? Preventative medicine at its very best is just around the corner, of your sleeve ...

Wave Learning 6.0 Trends

Wave 6.0 is all about learning, and it's interesting to see just how fast practical technology is moving in the machine learning space. There are things that have been announced since the first draft of this book. One example is a recent blog post from Tesla, effectively telling us that the learning ability of the Tesla fleet means its vehicles are going to teach each other to drive better than you can.

Then there's the rise of the intelligent virtual assistant. The new apps from companies including Google, Apple, Microsoft, Amazon, Viv, and many more are getting better and better at understanding human language and interacting with us in an increasingly natural way. The Advanced machine learning algorithms that drive these apps mean that they are improving themselves really quickly.

It won't be long, two to three years is my educated guess, before we will be using these virtual assistants to do all kinds of tasks for us. Fancy a night out? You will probably be able to ask your virtual butler to arrange a taxi, book the table of your favourite restaurant and buy your tickets to the movie. It's looking increasingly likely that your personal money will be run through one of these companies, and the costs of all of those things will be deducted from the budget that you give them. The tech company that wins this race is likely to get a tiny slice of a very big pie of your spending in the future. We already have Google Assistant, Amazon's Alexa, and speech recognition software becoming almost as accurate as a human listener.

What we haven't been able to reproduce so far is an accurate computer-generated representation of human speech, but that's all about to change. Google's WaveNet[29] system is producing very highly-scored natural-sounding speech when tested on real people. Currently it still needs a huge amount of processing power so isn't going to be available in the next few months, but the technology is there and moving really fast.

And what about a computer's ability to listen? Boundaries are being pushed in this area too. According to the tech website *Futurism*, Google's DeepMind AI can outperform human lip readers.[30] The article's summaries read: 'Google's DeepMind AI was able to correctly annotate

---

[29] http://www.theverge.com/2016/9/9/12860866/google-deepmind-wavenet-ai-text-to-speech-synthesis

[30] https://futurism.com/watch-your-mouth-googles-deepmind-ai-can-outperform-professional-lip-readers/

46.8% of words in a dataset without any mistakes compared to the 12.4% annotated by a human lip-reading professional,' and 'Advanced AI lip-reading systems could lead to improved hearing aids or allow for silent dictation in public spaces and speech recognition in noisy environments.'

Yannis Assael, a doctoral student at Oxford University in England, told *New Scientist* magazine[31] of his optimism for the usefulness of the technology: 'We believe that machine lip readers have enormous practical potential, with applications in improved hearing aids, silent dictation in public spaces, and speech recognition in noisy environments.' That technology has the ability to transform the way we interact with the smart machines playing an ever-increasing role in our lives. It might be a trivial example, but just imagine being able to almost silently whisper to your phone to turn your oven on at home and turn up the heating in time for you to get home before you leave your last meeting of the day. That's a reality that's going to be with us very quickly.

The Deep Code of Beautiful Music

Algorithms have even managed to crack the code of the music by famous composer Johann Sebastian Bach. Two scientists, Gaetan Hadjeres and Francois Pachet, from Sony Computer Science Laboratories trained a neural network they called DeepBach to learn and reproduce choral music based on an artificial intelligence system that had 'learned' how Bach himself had written this music. The resulting compositions fooled many professional musicians and music students. The same Sony lab also developed a system that could learn the music styles of a huge database of songs. Their FlowMachines system composed the first-ever entire song using AI, and published the results to YouTube[32] and SoundCloud.

Deep Learning Speeds Up

By using machine learning we are increasingly able to decode the miracles of nature and the patterns that have always been around us, but that until now we didn't have the processing power and intelligence to decode. But

---

[31] https://www.newscientist.com/article/2113299-googles-deepmind-ai-can-lip-read-tv-shows-better-than-a-pro

[32] https://youtu.be/LSHZ_b05W7o

now we can, if we take things step-by-step. I think it's likely that the human body will eventually be able to be 'reprogrammed' back into a healthy state. That's not as far-fetched as you might think.

In October 2016 Chris Bishop, head of Microsoft Research's Cambridge-based lab, told *Fast Company*, 'The field of biology and the field of computation might seem like chalk and cheese, but the complex processes that happen in cells have some similarity to those that happen in a standard desktop computer.' Microsoft have stated that they want to use their 'biological computation unit' to solve cancer within ten years.

Then there's the work of Brendan Frey. Frey is a co-founder of Deep Genomics and a professor at the University of Toronto and co-founder of its Machine Learning Group; he decided to focus on his specialist area after learning, in 2002, that his unborn baby had a genetic problem. Frey told a reporter: 'I wanted to use machine learning to improve the lives of hundreds of millions of people facing similar genetic challenges. Second, reducing uncertainty is tremendously valuable; giving someone news, either good or bad, lets them plan accordingly.'[33]

Frey's work at the forefront of genome and machine learning technology puts him in a strong position to make predictions. The torrents of data in the field have been difficult to deal with until recently, but Frey believes that soon you will be able to sequence your genome using a cell-phone-sized device for less than a trip to the corner store. He goes on: 'The genome is only part of the story; there exists huge amounts of data that describe cells and tissues. We, as humans, can't quite grasp all this data; we don't yet know enough biology. Machine learning can help solve the problem.'

Living in a 6.0 World – Learning in 2030

Imagine it is 2030. Today, it's quite normal to communicate with your computer in the same way you communicate with normal humans. You can use natural language, show your emotions, and use gestures – and your computer understands you.

Life can sometimes feel more like a scene from the Will Smith version of the Isaac Asimov novel *I, Robot*. Machine learning software has developed so fast in the last decade that our computers have been learning at an exponential rate. It means that they're able to have a level of advanced

---

[33] https://www.oreilly.com/ideas/deep-learning-meets-genome-biology

sensory perception that's getting close to ours. Our computers can now interpret visual, auditory, and tactile information in such a natural way that it's now perfectly normal for us to expect them to be able to process things like we can.

Our modern machine learning algorithms have enabled us to create all kinds of smart software and hardware tools; tools that have made our lives easier than ever and even more convenient. Our organisations, and even our families, have been able to use these amazing machine learning algorithms to learn and solve some really complex problems. As a result our homes, our transport vehicles, our personal devices, our companies, and just about everything we come into contact with has become exponentially smarter.

Back in the early 2020s, machines where finally able to learn from humans, and in the process our machines started to adapt to us more and more. Now our technology actually understands our true human needs. It has been able to adapt to us by adopting behaviours that are ever more human and more natural for us to be around. We are so well taken care of that we have finally had the foresight to look beyond ourselves.

Our energy needs were met long ago when we were able to harness the energy from the sun. Thankfully, use of fossil fuels died out a long time ago and it created the space for us to breathe clearly and to think clearly. The balance of world power shifted because we were no longer beholden to a few big corporates (or governments) with a stranglehold on our energy needs.

When we were all able to choose to be 'off-grid' whenever we wanted to be, we had time to start caring about the world around us; the world that sustained us.

Our learning revolution also had a profound impact on the way that we lived and worked. We were finally about to shake off the last of the Industrial Revolution back in the mid-2020s.

So the question now is this: What next? What needs do we still have? Well, that question was the one that, all those years ago, so interested Abraham Maslow. Remember his pyramid? Right at the top was the ultimate in human expression, the very essence of self. Right at the top is our own need for self-actualisation; our need to create, our need for the ultimate in purpose and the self-expression of our very humanity. Our future lies in a sense of purpose that defines who we are.

The Big Catalyst

The machine learning revolution sped up everything, more and more machines became autonomous and machines started to understand and speak a more human-style natural language.

Machine learning impacted all the five layers and waves below. It changed how we manage and organise our communities, how we design and manage our infrastructure, how we structure our information networks, how we develop our apps and automation solutions, and how we share information, assets, and trust.

Machine learning affected so many layers at the same time, and so deeply, that many traditional institutes couldn't keep up with the exponential speed of change. Change became an understatement; 'radical transformation' became a better description. Many of these organisations disappeared from the map somewhere between 2017 and 2030.

The new organisations that were founded during the learning wave were highly adaptable as organisations; learning was in their DNA from the start. Machine learning algorithms were the core business of these new companies. Everything they did was based on fast learning and being highly adaptable. The generation of highly adaptive organisations that were founded during the machine learning revolution had the highest probability of surviving into the next decade. Today in 2030, companies are not the companies we know from the past, and today we see that many of our communities have been empowered by machine learning technology. It gets easier to coordinate the complexity and everything does seem to run more smoothly.

Focused Intelligence

Machine learning changed everything about the way we solve problems. At the beginning of the learning revolution we used machine learning in the same way as the first organisms used their neocortex. We used it to develop simple tools that made our lives more convenient; tools that solved all kinds of problems and even tools that developed even better and faster tools. This first form of intelligence we called 'Artificial Narrow Intelligence'.

But the real impact of machine learning systems really hit home when our learning systems became so powerful that we were finally about to decode the clues that nature gave us. Nature took millions of years to solve some very complex problems. The solutions had been surrounding us all the time, but we just hadn't been able to decode the clues nature had given us. We hadn't had the power to understand what was right in front of our eyes.

What is the algorithm behind managing a community of billions of individual cells? What is the algorithm behind the smell of a dog? What is the algorithm behind the advanced logistics system that transports billions of blood cells and nutrients through the veins of an organism? What is the algorithm behind the energy management within the human body? What is the algorithm behind the working of the human brain?

The more powerful machine learning systems opened our eyes and turned Nature's clues into natures answers.

Today in 2030 we have a better understanding than ever before of how Nature operates and how she solves problems on a molecular and cellular level. As a result, humanity started to mimic Nature more and more. We have learned how to 'grow' computer chips using advanced crystallisation technology inspired by nature. We have learned to grow new materials that are super-strong and super-conductive, by using principles she showed us.

We learned to look to nature first. After all, why invent solutions for problems while she has already solved almost every complex problem that we can imagine? Nature took millions of years to solve them and came up with elegant and efficient solutions. The only thing we needed to do was decode the structures and patterns nature provided us with. We finally unlocked the gift.

> 'Look deep into nature, and then you will understand
> everything better.'
>
> – Albert Einstein

In the past decade, we have used the incredible pattern recognition to solve humanity's most urgent problems, including our energy problems, resource limitations, our logistics challenges, our communication challenges, our community organisation problems, and even most of our health problems.

We gained a deep understanding about matter and energy that led us to propulsion and energy systems that we could not have dreamed of a decade earlier.

'Everything you can imagine, nature has already created.'
– Albert Einstein

Our powerful machine learning algorithms, combined with powerful quantum computers, are unlocking the very mystery of life and consciousness itself. Every day we are gaining a deeper insight into our world and the universe we live in. We are finally starting to grasp what consciousness really is and how it works.

The more deeply we decode our universe, the more human we become and the greater understanding we have of the very the essence of our being.

Democratised Intelligence

Our machines that used machine learning themselves became exponentially better at specific tasks. They became much faster and much better than humans ever could be! But in the early days, the tasks they excelled at were mostly very narrow and very specific.

After we mastered machine learning systems and developed many focused/narrow intelligence applications (intelligent tools for specific tasks), we realised that we could connect and combine these narrow intelligences into more general intelligent applications. These combined intelligences work like the search engines of today (Google and Bing). Search engines were indexing webpages with information so they were able to redirect people with questions to specific website. The general intelligences of today work in a similar way, and have developed them into artificial identities. These intelligence engines are indexing intelligence and themselves tap into many modular narrow intelligence solutions and combine them into one general intelligent identity.

So instead of just having a 'search engine' for information we have more of an 'intelligence engine' that taps into available, standardised sources of intelligence. These artificial identities are already helping us to solve all kinds of problems. Some of these intelligence sources are free, and some are commercial intelligence sources with very specific intelligences that are very valuable indeed. Back in 2016 we had app stores; now in 2030 we have intelligence stores where you can buy/rent all kinds of intelligences. The more intelligence modules you activate, the more intelligence you can access and the more problems you can solve.

Human-level Intelligence is Coming

Back in 2016, many people (including big-hitting thinkers like Steven Hawkins, Elon Musk, Bill Gates, and others) were afraid of artificial super intelligence and very vocal about it.

They were posing questions that focused on issues such as, what if intelligences increase their intelligence exponentially and eventually make the human race obsolete?

What if these 'entities' improve themselves so quickly and become more intelligent than all of us combined, might they eventually decide that people aren't useful and decide to get rid of us altogether? But if we look at the 'learning wave' in biology, Nature tells us a different story. Were the cells in our body destroyed by our neocortex brains? Did our brains make our cells obsolete? No, instead, the opposite happened. Our cloud-shaped brains (similar to our machine learning algorithms in the cloud) empowered our individual cells by keeping the entire organism (our system) healthy and away from danger. All cells in our body benefited and our brain helped us to improve our entire quality of life. We adapted to our environment even faster, we stayed safe from harm, and our survivability increased.

Humanification Predicts ...

I believe that by 2030 we will see the first general intelligences reach a human level of artificial intelligence. We will also see the first artificial intelligence that's able to reprogramme and optimise itself to the point where it will become even more intelligent. I think we are going to see AI solving problems beyond the scope that they were even built for.

We are going to be using AI to improve the quality of our lives, increase our overall safety, our health, our communication, our collaboration, the coherence of our communities, and the efficiency of our energy and infrastructure.

In other words, these intelligent entities are going to help us to focus on the top of the Maslow pyramid. That's going to allow us to focus on our passions, our purpose, and our fulfilment.

That's where we go next. That's what Wave 7.0 is all about. Are you ready for the ride of your life? Because it's just around the corner ...

Chapter 36

Wave 7.0 –
The Future of Creation

The 7th Wave – The Ultimate Expression

Our brain's prefrontal cortex enables us to imagine things and execute specific tasks.

Our ancestors started to use their prefrontal cortex to develop advanced language. That was the start of us having shared ideas and then it became the cradle of our very civilisation and the start of our human culture.

I believe that we will use the virtual equivalent of our prefrontal cortex brain (our collective accumulation of artificial intelligence) to use our collective imagination as a group. That's going to give us the power to bring to life the ideas formed from our collective intelligence. Increasingly the imagination of people and the use of AI will blend and become almost seamless and that will give us the speed and the knowledge to bring our dreams to life and reach solutions that have, up until now, been unimaginable.

If we mirror the patterns of Nature, then as our collective intelligence matures, we as a society will start to increasingly reflect on ourselves and have the tools to do something useful with what we discover.

That gives me great hope that we will have the power and the will to solve bigger and bigger problems and realise our needs to understand the world around us and ultimately gain true insight into ourselves.

Our creative process will help us to create new things that are dematerialised and decentralised. From cars to buildings, from cities to space stations, in the future I believe they will all be co-creations of the crowd. Humanity is going to have the power to use its shared imagination, shared decision-making, and the miracle of co-creation. But for the time being, there is one big hurdle for you, and that is that there is only one of you. The question is, will that always be the case? We have been fantasising about avatars and playing around with the principle for a long time. But are we about to get closer to truly replicating ourselves? Are humans themselves about to go virtual as part of Wave 7.0 . . .?

The Rise and Rise of Creative Platforms

During Wave 7.0 we are going to have very powerful technology at our fingertips. All the technology from Wave 1.0 to Wave 6.0 will still be there, and it will be more automated, intuitive, and user-friendly than ever before.

Almost all of us are going to have access to powerful platforms that will lift and amplify our creative and social capabilities. I believe that a creative revolution far beyond anything we can currently imagine is going to be unleashed.

We have already seen the beginning of the 5.0 wave of social sharing in the form of social media. I'm confident that we are going to see even bigger and exponentially more powerful platforms in the learning wave. These platforms are going to enable ordinary people to do some extraordinary things.

Sadly, many companies will fall, but there will be a saving grace. At the same time, many more online platforms are going to empower more and more people to earn a living without needing a company or government to take care of them.

I'm fundamentally optimistic that some of these platforms are going to end up transferring jobs and revenue from the big institutions to millions of people all over the world instead, providing a decent direct income.

Look at Uber – if you have a car and a driving licence you can earn money as a taxi driver. Or take Airbnb – when you have a spare room, you can earn money. These platforms are rapidly becoming great enablers for millions of people. If you have a good idea you can use Kickstarter to fund it, or you can use Quirky to get expert help to design and produce a product, even when you don't have the skills yourself.

There are video bloggers that have their own TV channel on YouTube and earn millions of dollars by posting content. These are all examples of opportunities that weren't even imaginable to the mass market just a decade ago.

I'm far from being the only person to believe that a world of meaningful work is the way that we are headed. Back in 2015, Ray Kurzweil, the inventor, author, futurologist, and a founding trustee of Singularity University, stated: 'I'm actually not worried about it [the demise of 9-5 employment] because it's going to ultimately be very easy and require a very small fraction of our output to support all the material needs of the human race.'[34]

I agree, and the move towards a world of meaningful work and a life of purpose for more and more of us is the core message of optimism that I wanted to share by writing this book.

---

[34] https://singularityhub.com/2016/08/23/the-end-of-meaningless-jobs-will-unleash-the-worlds-creativity/

Chapter 37
Wave 7.0 – Trends

Shared Creativity and Decision-making

There are already some exciting developments in this area. We have been using the idea of swarms of humans and how we behave as a group for some time when we have been planning urban spaces and traffic systems, for example. But already there are scientists taking the idea of the swarm much further. Think of swarm intelligence as an elevated intelligence that's a collection of knowledge and insights from a pool of real human minds. Unanimous AI have developed UNU, a swarm intelligence[35] technology that allows groups to combine their thoughts and feelings in real time. People can answer questions, make decisions, or just enjoy themselves by being together. UNU 'Has been designed to unleash the brainpower of groups, combining their knowledge, opinions, and instincts into a Swarm Intelligence that is often smarter and more insightful than the individuals would be alone'.

Between the first draft of this book and the final one, there have been some interesting things that have come from UNU, not least of which the almost superhuman power of prediction that the platform had in 2016.[36] UNU predicted the winner of the Kentucky Derby, the Super Bowl, forecast many of the Oscar winners, the winner of the Stanley Cup, and now, the full post-season of major-league baseball in the United States.

Then there's data analytics firm Quid,[37] which helps users to 'Query, map, and explore massive amounts of information at one time.' The Quid application indexes millions of documents and creates an interactive visual map of the data. In layman's terms, it turns data into pictures of the news and opinions of people on particular topics. It allows forecasters to

---

[35] http://unu.ai
[36] https://futurism.com/harnessing-the-power-of-the-hive-mind-has-allowed-one-company-to-predict-the-future/
[37] https://www.quid.com

navigate through the world's collective intelligence and see relationships that were previously hidden and answer strategic questions. Simply, it's the thinking of the swarm revealed.

What about Emotionally Intelligent (EI) products? Then why not grab yourself a database of emotions? That's already a reality, and it's going to be a trend that's going to grow and grow, in my view. A Massachusetts based company, Affectiva[38] uses computer vision and deep learning technology to analyse facial expressions or non-verbal cues in visual content online, and the co-founder, Rana el Kiliouby, claims that the system can add EI and empathy to any interactive product. Want insights into how your customers are reacting to your product? No problem, just let Affectiva watch their reactions! Or there's Beyond Verbal, a company that can give 'Emotions Analytics' that will enable your devices to interact with you on an emotional level. Beyond Verbal[39] say they have technology that can identify people's moods from their voices. Designed primary, it seems, for commercial use, the tech features emotion analytics technology that doesn't even consider the content or context of the spoken word itself. It looks for emotions instead and can detect signs of anger, anxiety, arousal, and more by studying the intonation in a person's voice. The company even suggests call centres could also use the technology to improve relationships between operators and customers. They aren't the only kids on that particular block either: there's the B2C app SONIPHI,[40] a soon-to-be-launched voice analysis app that reveals your body's health, well-being, and mood in real time through the use of dynamic voice analysis to 'help you achieve optimal vitality'.

The general trend here is that technology is going to get better and better at reading us and responding in a way that is going to get more and more human until our interactions with it become almost seamless. It is up to us how far we want that seamlessness to go.

You – Gone Digital

You and Your Digital Double

For the final time in our journey into the future together, it's time to teleport yourself to another year. It's 2030, and you have a double. A Digital Double. A digital version of you.

---

[38] http://www.affectiva.com
[39] http://www.beyondverbal.com
[40] http://www.soniphi.com

A Digital Double is a mirror presence of you that lives exclusively in cyberspace. A virtual you; without actually being you.

Your Digital Double thinks like you, buys like you, communicates like you, answers messages like you, gathers information like you, makes connections like you, makes decisions like you.

But this isn't simply something pretending to be you. Oh no, it's way more than that. Your Digital Double is like a virtual extension of your prefrontal cortex; it can visualise things for you, it can create things for you, and it can make decisions for you in the digital domain.

For the twenty-five years between 2005 and today, all the interactions between you and the internet have been tracked, recorded, and stored in detail on massive data servers. Every search you made, every purchase you decided to make, every browser button you idly pressed, every transaction you did, every tweet you sent, every email you wrote, every social media post you created, every blog post you wrote, every photo you took, every YouTube video you loaded, every geographical location you visited, and even website you visited was tracked and stored in huge databases.

When, sometime around 2021, tech got smart enough to do something useful with the data, the smart machine learning algorithms had enough to 're-create' you. They learned from each interaction you made with the digital world. These smart algorithms made your digital profile even more personal, accurate, and even filled the gaps to create a perfect foundation for your Digital Double.

Due to a recently introduced privacy law, all this personal data is now owned and controlled by you. The advent of Fluid Quantum Encryption technology saw to that.

Today, you even have the ability to add intelligence and authority to that profile so it can act as your Digital Double in the digital world with data that wasn't collected elsewhere. In other words, you were able to bring your (relatively dumb and uneducated) personal profile data to life by adding both real and artificial smartness and autonomy to your passive and reactive profile data. Genius.

In the first few months, your Digital Double started in test mode and at first you were only able to use it for things that didn't have any dire consequences if it went wrong. After all, it was always going to take a little while for you to teach your Digital Double how to behave in certain situations and how to act in the digital world in a way that truly represented who you are. As your double became more mature (after a couple of months of intensive use), you got more and more confident to allow it to make formal transactions and act as a legal person that represented you in the virtual world.

It was amazing how quickly it picked things up and became a truly authentic digital version of you. It became a joy to allow it to buy your clothes for you and even go to meetings. Wow, how those meetings used to bore you; now you only have to attend the ones that feed your mind and soul. As it fully matured, the really fun part started!

Your Digital Double has one enormous advantage: it can be in multiple places at the same time. So, for example, it earns money (or some social currency or credits) for you in multiple places at the same time. On top of that, you Digital Double participates in co-creation communities, teaches other people's Digital Doubles specific skills or knowledge that you have, and there's a growing market for Digital Double skills. You can, say, buy in a skill so it can write a book for you or edit a movie for you.

Like the voice in your head, your Digital Double will reflect on things for you and give you advice for the real world, and vice versa. If your Digital Double isn't sure about something it simply asks before it pops back over to cyberspace and takes action for you.

A couple of years after the introduction of your Digital Double, the system got a major update, with a brand new user interface. Non-invasive brain tracking devices which tracked your brain activity became available, so for the first time you were able to communicate with the digital world on a thought level. This improvement had huge implications, because from that moment onwards there were no limits; no bandwidth limits, and no spoken and written language to slow things down.

And while your Digital Double is very busy in the virtual world, often at 1,000 places at the same time (because you are very in demand these days), you can enjoy life to the fullest in the real world. Your Digital Double deals with the official and boring stuff so you don't have to. Life is much more fun.

In short, your Digital Double is a virtual extension of your brain's prefrontal cortex, on steroids! It's a virtual extension of you and a firewall to protect the real you from digital attack. But the best part of all is that the true you gets be more human in the real world.

Last Minute Update: Just before this book went to press.

According to Gartner at the end of 2016, digital twins for things is just around the corner. Gartner, a technology research and advisory company, have forecasted that within three to five years, billions of things will be represented by digital twins. They describe this as 'a dynamic software model of a physical thing or system'. They go on to say:

> Using physics data on how the components of a thing operate and respond to the environment as well as data provided by sensors in the physical world, a digital twin can be used to analyse and simulate real world conditions, respond to changes, improve operations and add value.

It is interesting that parallel processing is also going on in the world of ideas around identity. Although Gartner hadn't taken things as far as digitised versions of ourselves, this forecast[41] of digital twins that function as proxies for the combination of skilled individuals and traditional monitoring devices and controls is one step closer to the very idea of digital doubles that you just read about – text I wrote some time before the Gartner trends report. The data firm quite rightly acknowledge that there is a big cultural shift required to implement digital twins (even for devices) but go on to hint at even further developments in the pipeline:

> Digital twins of physical assets combined with digital representations of facilities and environments as well as people, businesses and processes will enable an increasingly detailed digital representation of the real world for simulation, analysis and control.

It's a small step by a big company, but it's heading towards the digitisation of humans and it's up to us to work together to get that right.

Collective Consciousness and Hive Minds

If all the patterns play out, (and there's no reason to believe they won't) by 2030, increasing technology will have pushed humanity so far forward so quickly that traditional, centralised decision-making structures simply won't work anymore.

Instead, there's likely to be a different sort of power and decision-making structure. I believe the most likely alternative will be a strong grid or network structure that distributes the power to make changes equally. By spreading the pressure points you get huge advantages. By using the power of many minds you get a greater distribution of

---

41 http://www.gartner.com/smarterwithgartner/gartners-top-10-technology-trends-2017/

responsibility. In many ways it makes sense. A coherent network of people is able to handle a lot more stress and pressure than one individual, or small group of individuals, can. The coherency itself distributes and balances the power equally over the network. We needed decision-making networks to keep our society moving forward.

Decision-making platforms use the brainpower of groups. By combining the knowledge, opinions, and instincts of each member of the group with technology to make sense of the whole we have the opportunity to tap into a kind of swarm intelligence that is smarter and more insightful than individuals working in isolation.

Decision-making platforms are not simply an online community with a bunch of people in it. Good decision-making platforms are highly advanced software platforms that mobilise people in a structured way. By enabling people to act together like they are one single organism we are able to see a future where the best decisions are made that advance the whole of humanity by using our collective intelligence.

These platforms facilitate long-term relationships between individuals, and with the help of advanced algorithms and tools they will empower those people to make genuinely shared decisions. Decision-making platforms will change and improve many areas of our society. From very small decisions on a local level to very big decisions on a global level, decision-making platforms will help us to handle a fast-changing world and adapt more, with greater speed.

After the introduction of Digital Doubles, decision-making and governance changed even more dramatically.

Before the Digital Doubles, the decision-making networks running on maximum speed were limited to the speed of human reactions. That was because within the platform you needed a critical mass of people to make critical choices. But when people were allowed to let their Digital Double participate these decision-making networks, things started to speed up really fast. Decisions can now be made at the speed of light.

Millions (and later billions) of Digital Doubles from all over the world represented the decisions and choices of an equal number of real humans in the real world. Real-time direct democracy was born; a lightning-fast democracy that could run in real time and take the decisions and opinions of billions of humans into account.

The decision-making platform based on Digital Doubles, then, mirrors Nature and behaves in the same way as one giant, shared virtual prefrontal cortex for the whole of humanity.

Wave 7.0 – Shared Imagination

Holographic collaboration

I believe that more and more co-visualisation and co-creation platforms will soon be powered by advanced AI technology. That is going to be able to leverage and boost the creativity and productivity of our global community even more, and we will be participating in an ever-greater collective consciousness.

This is going to make designing and working together easier than ever. We will be able to use holograms to work together. We will probably be using mixed reality devices like the Microsoft HoloLens[42] (but a hundred thousand times better if the we follow the S-curve), and that's going to enable collaboration with people all over the world. We are going to be able to work on products that are virtual, and everyone working on it will be able to visualise the product in the same way at the same time and be able to interact with it. Country barriers will drop away and our desire to act for the common good will take over. Scientists from many countries have collaborated across borders for many years and, finally, the rest of us will be able to do the same.

A Trip to 2030

By 2030 many companies and organisations have already transitioned into using co-visualisation and co-creation platforms. In other words, the era of the hive mind arrived and the idea of coherent communities of highly motivated individuals became a reality. Now we design and build complex things together and share the benefits in fairer ways and have the opportunity to do work for good causes. Traditional centralised company structures died because they weren't able to change fast enough; they couldn't stay relevant for their target audience. The death of the global corporate was a shock to many, but people in the world of technology weren't surprised at all; they had been predicting it for years.

Back in 2015 machine learning revolutionised the product design industry. With generative design, we witnessed the first genuine co-creation between humans and machines. At the beginning of the co-creation revolution, machine learning enabled designers to be better

---

[42] https://youtu.be/aThCr0PsyuA

designers, but fast-forward to 2030 everybody can be a designer! It used to be the case that product designers needed a deep understanding of materials, shapes, and strength calculations. They had to think about each tiny part of the product. But now we have smart design software. Like many things, it's powered by machine learning algorithms and the crowd makes everyone a product designer. If you want to design something, all you have to do is tell the platform what you would like to have as a product and the software starts to design it right away.

The software presents you with a wide range of possible 3D design outcomes and you can explore the design proposal in mixed reality. You can even see the product projected as a hologram, where you can interact and play with it as if it already existed. You have the freedom to choose which design direction you like the most, and the software incorporates all your feedback and creates a new version of your design until the product exactly meets your needs. Want to involve others too? Well you can ... You simply ask other community members from the co-creation platform and they are there to help you craft the best product possible. Everyone has an opinion; that's not something that's ever changed!

The co-creation revolution started with simple and small products like small electronic devices, furniture, and design products. But soon the products designed and created by these co-creation communities became more advanced and complex. As confidence grew, the first electric 3D-printed cars were on the agenda, and it didn't take long for other vehicles to follow: drones to transport people and even rockets to explore outer space. Also, homes were entirely designed and built by the community and for the community. Off-grid home designs were shared on the web as an open-source model, and more and more people started to use them.

When the model of designing and creating homes together was proven to be safe and super-efficient, it didn't take long for other types of building to follow.

Digital Double's enabled a lot of new possibilities that weren't thinkable before. People wanted to be involved in the design and creation of new things, and by around the year 2030 almost all the things that can be designed and built will be designed and built by some kind of co-creation platform. It won't be long before we master homes, cars, drones, and toys and move on to see our co-creation communities (powered by smart software) designing space stations and even entirely new civilisations in outer space. Until now it was only possible for humans to participate in co-creation communities, but from now on Digital Doubles will be able to participate and help to make design decisions. Just imagine the speed of progress then.

Part 3

How to Adapt, Innovate and Thrive

Humanification in the Real World

The Speed of Change

There are some interesting things about the timing of waves that we haven't talked about yet. The big one is that all 7.0 waves inside an S-curve don't all take the same amount of time.

Think of the waves as tracks 1–7 on an old-style long-playing vinyl record. As the turntable spins, the outer tracks have long revolutions, but as the needle gets closer to the hole in the centre of the record, the needle makes faster and faster revolutions. It's not because the turntable is going

Fibonacci Curve

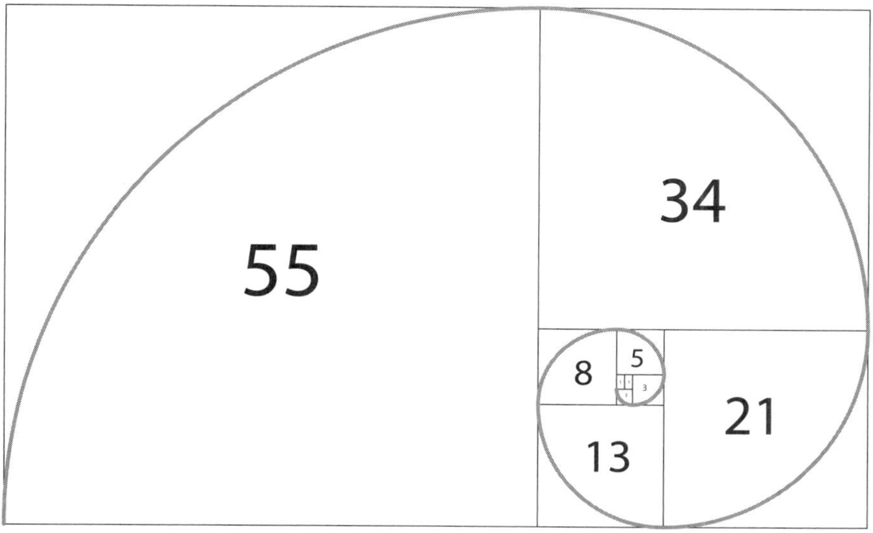

Figure 7: Nature follows spiral curves, from atoms all the way to galaxies.

faster but because the needle has to travel less and less distance the closer to the end of the record it gets. The spiral of travel gets ever smaller as you get closer to the conclusion. So it is with life.

The first multicellular cells jumped on to the record hundreds of millions of years ago. At first they started to glide very slowly around the outside of the record. The first track took hundreds of millions of years to play. The second track, where Nature starts to help things along by creating some infrastructure, plays a little faster, but still it takes tens of millions of years to complete. At every turn of the record, the time and distance the needle has to travel to get it closer to the middle of the disc gets a little shorter, and so it is for every wave in the cycle.

By the time we get to track (Wave) 7.0, the final track only takes 100,000 years to play. Wave 7.0 is the music of humans. Track 7 is our song.

The single cells that evolved to advanced cell communities, which we now call communities of human beings, are still developing. But there is no doubt that we are getting close to the centre of the record. How many more new records are there to play? Who knows? Only our imagination can show us what's possible.

It takes more and more stability now for the needle to stay stable as the speed of the record increases. There is more room for disruption the closer to the centre of the record you get because as the speed increases and the turns become smaller, the outward forces that want to throw you off the rail have become exponentially bigger. That is why organisations and products have (and will continue to) become more and more virtual. It's just a physical reality that virtual organisations and products have less weight and are less affected by the centrifugal forces – or even not affected at all.

Becoming virtual is the only way to withstand the exponentially growing centrifugal force. If you are weightless, the physical forces don't affect you at all. The new disruptive organisations that are already household names – like Uber, Airbnb, and Skype – became virtual companies without any physical assets. That's why these organisations have been able to keep the music playing. Organisations with virtual products (like software, data, algorithms, and services) are most capable of keeping up with the exponential speed of change because they aren't going to get flung off to the side as the music speeds up. They will simply be able to change their tune.

New Weightless Organisations

Quantum Innovation Waves – A Paradigm Shift in Developmental Thinking Is Needed

The big challenge here is simple. How do we speed up the innovation cycle to keep up with the pace of technology change?

And why is that so important anyway?

Well, let's deal with the issue of the importance of speed first. If you have technology that's changing on a rapid cycle, and your product development is slow, then by the time you have got your tech widget to market the technology that is at the heart of it is already out of date!

As we move through the wave we are in at the moment at a faster and faster pace, with the constant doubling, we need to develop our products at a faster and faster rate than ever before. So here's the million-dollar question:

How on earth do we do that?

Switching Our Thinking

Simple. You just think big, but start small.

Mostly, that's not how we work at the moment. Generally, we come from a culture of thinking big and starting big. That thinking is the legacy of large corporate culture that dominated through the twentieth century. But today, the numerous old-style checks and balances that many people are used to no longer apply; they take too long and they stifle innovation and creative thinking, so we need to adapt our product development cycle accordingly.

So what's got to change? Well, first of all we need to stop thinking so big at the beginning. Thinking big and starting big generates a lot of stuff that has to be managed. You get functional documents and designs and all sorts of other documents around the project. Then you give those documents to ten different people and each of the ten people have a different perception of the project!

Things get super complicated really quickly, so the next thing you need is yet another layer of decision-making so you can wade through all the options. But it doesn't have to be like that. There is another way: A better way.

Instead, you build a small prototype – very small – and give it to a number of people who are your ideal user or target customer.

Every person sees exactly the same prototype and they react to it. The result? You get much more actionable feedback, and that feedback comes in at a much faster rate. It also really helps to break down the project into very small pieces at each stage of the process. You start with very small blocks, and you start with the blocks with the highest risks attached.

So you develop the idea into a prototype before you get bogged down in lots of options – they can come later if the prototype shows promise with users. If the prototype doesn't work, then your entire idea won't work, because the prototype is the foundation of your entire idea. Using this fast-track method, you can build your product out much faster and gather more feedback than you can using traditional models.

I believe that it's also really important to focus on human needs and to connect to people on a much higher level than we do today. We have been traditionally educated to think in rigid terms of personas, demographics, and traditional target audiences. Instead, I believe that smart people in high-performing organisations will learn to think in terms of personal needs or spiritual needs instead. So how do we create things that deliver to the personal needs of our customers and communities at a deeper level?

To answer that question, it helps to look at the work of some human behaviour experts (people like Tony Robbins), who have turned their thinking towards our deeper human needs instead of our simple material wants. Many businesses who have looked at their interactions from this perspective have totally transformed how they message and communicate with their customers and, as a result, have seen huge growth and benefits to their customers.

Robbins adapted and simplified Maslow's original pyramid into six human needs that any organisation can refer to in order to understand how their product or service will serve the end user in a way that goes beyond the material, and that's got to be good for business.

These needs include:

1. **Certainty** – We all need to feel in control and to know what's coming over the horizon. We all need a feeling of knowing what's coming next so we can feel secure and function at our best. It's a survival mechanism that helps us decide how much risk we're willing to take in life. The higher the need for certainty people have, the fewer risks that those people are willing to take.
2. **Variety** – If things are too certain, you'd get very bored! Variety really is the spice of life. We all enjoy good surprises; the bad

surprises are what we call our problems! Variety keeps us alert and helps us grow. You often see people whose lives are filled with certainty (for example, enjoying huge success or wealth) taking greater and greater risks like climbing mountains, greater business risks, and adrenaline sports, or gambling to feed their need for variety. Robbins sometimes refers to this as our need for uncertainty.

3. **Significance** – Everybody has a need to feel important, special, unique, or needed, and people express that need in lots of different ways. Sometimes, negativity can give people significance; being constantly sick or having bigger problems than other people certainly keeps you being noticed! Some people express it more positively by earning lots of money, inventing something groundbreaking, achieving academic excellence, or by growing a massive social media network.

4. **Love and connection** – We all need these two things on some level. Humans need to be loved and to connect with others. Some people connect with animals or objects (who hasn't mourned when we lose something dear to us – even a favourite item of clothing?). Humans get attached to things and we love each other. It's at the core of our being.

5. **Growth** – We all need to feel like we are moving forward in life at some level. We can do it by expanding our minds or doing something that adds to the greater sum of human (or our own) experience. Whole industries are based on our need for growth: education, sporting achievement, academia, science, research. And for many of us the way we make our living is a big part of our personal growth.

6. **Contribution** – Nearly all of us have an intrinsic need to give back at some level. Just think about it. When you get some good news, it's likely you want to call somebody you love and share it with them. By sharing, you enhance everything you experience in your life and it helps you to create meaning. Ultimately, it's not what you get that will make you happy long-term, but rather who you become and what you contribute that will impact how fulfilled you feel.

For companies to be successful, it's important that the development of new products and services includes a focus on these personal needs as well as the practical benefits. By understanding what we, as human beings, are really looking for out of life, we can build better products and be more successful. This understanding will help build great marketing campaigns too.

All of these needs affect what we do in life to earn a living, or play our part in life. We all have a slightly different combination and hierarchy of preferences. Some people like more certainty, and they tend to become employees. Some people crave more variety, and they tend to become entrepreneurs because they have a higher desire and tolerance for risk, and we need risk-takers in organisations too – if we don't have them there's little innovation and very little testing or new marketing experiments.

Everybody has certain precepts and a different balance of these needs. If you talk to people at the level of these more value-based ideas, then you are going to connect on a much higher level with the people. Your customers will connect with your products better and your teams will connect with your vision too.

'Why' is a Massive Driver

What I see more is that people are getting more aware of the bigger reasons behind their buying decisions. People are making conscious choices about their activities and purchasing habits based on a values match with the supplier. They want the purposes of supplier and customer to have a match – or a feeling of one at least. One of the early pioneers of 'why'-based business was Anita Roddick in the UK who started Body Shop (later bought be L'Oreal), who was in business to provide microbusiness opportunities to people overseas and a conscience purchase that supported fair trade and animal-testing-free products on the high street. People bought into why Roddick was in business, and the purchase of the products naturally followed. It's always happened, but as marketing has become more sophisticated, people are noticing more and more when this value match is missing.

You have to intrinsically motivate people to use your product, and, therefore, you need to talk to them at an emotional level, on a feeling level, and you need loyal customers to have a business with a long-term future. When you find a way to do that, you're going to be able to connect on a much higher level than if you connect at product level alone.

More and more companies have started to do this. One example is Coca-Cola, who included the phrase 'open happiness' in a recent marketing campaign; they even used their entire marketing budget to help people who had been victims of an earthquake a couple of years ago.

Google talks about 'organizing the world's information'. These companies have a strong purpose that resonates with people.

With such massive intent and a clear sense of purpose it's much easier to attract the great employees, partners, and customers. A clear purpose works like a magnet for the right people. You attract them because they resonate with your bigger goals, your bigger purpose.

Making Your Products Accessible

If you want to build successful products, it's a constant mission to increase motivation and remove friction. If you are in the product development business, you need to continuously make your products more and more accessible, because our expectations are increasing all the time.

Remember how the iPad changed everything? Smart tech like that has also had the side effect of reducing our patience. For example, large intake forms to apply for things are long gone; forms are now reduced to one or two fields on a screen.

These are just a few examples of the same basic concept that when technology feels more natural people start to adopt it more easily – and they adopt it faster and they adopt it with less friction too.

Another thing people crave is a level of simplicity. If you make a graph with customer satisfaction on one axis and the amount of information or features people can cope with on the other axis, then what you see is there is a sweet spot on the upper side. The graph lines meet where the number of features is fairly small and satisfaction levels are high.

The iPad is a great example. You can do almost anything with it and it's really intuitive. That's what people are looking for. Make it relevant, make it simple, and give it a feeling of having been designed with some common sense.

So How Do You Design Products Like That?

It's simple, and your job is to keep it that way! You just start with a Minimum Viable Product and start to experiment.

A minimal viable product is a sort of prototype, and it's not a thin layer of functionality, rather it's a slice of your complete product, so emotional design, usability, reliability, and functionality is all included, but it's just a small slice. Test it with your target audience and then make the slice bigger and bigger based on real user feedback and not on your assumptions.

Using this type of lean start-up method, you transform your idea to a product or a service, create a prototype, and then you test it with your customers (or your target audience).

They react in a binary way: they hate it or they love it. If they hate it, it's back to the drawing board to search for other ways to meet their needs, but if they love it you persevere and build on what you already know. From there, you can move up and develop great products that people really want.

The Companies of the Future

As we move further through this current wave, more and more companies are going to become digital and weightless, supplying virtual products and virtual services. When I talk about digital or virtual products or services I'm talking, in most cases, about software and algorithms. More and more of the successful companies of the future are going to be creating and supplying us with intelligent solutions that have no physical presence.

When you develop products and services for human beings, you are going to have to get better and better at developing things that meet the needs, motivations, and behaviours of those human beings. This is true for the physical products of today, and it is going to be even more important for the virtual products and services that are going to make up a growing proportion of the things that we are going to buy and use in the future.

Today, we all have so many options to choose from, so why would any of us choose a product or service that does not meet 100% of our needs? Why would we even consider something that doesn't match up with our natural behaviour and our deepest motivations?

They are lofty goals indeed, and they lead to the all-important question for entrepreneurs and businesses:

How do you make sure you design and develop products that suit the needs of human beings?

Answer: Act like Nature does . . .

Sense and Simplicity to Inspire Natural Solutions

Nature solves everything in an elegant and efficient way. Everything in Nature has sense (although we might not understand it completely yet). In the natural world, nature solved the problem and found solutions in the most elegant and simple way imaginable. Nature has an inherent sense of simplicity that we can learn from.

A sense of simplicity is so important when we design any new business model, product, or service.

Why do you think Apple and Google are so successful? There are lots of other companies with the same technological skills; lots of other firms with great people working for them.

Successful companies like Google and Apple have created products that breathe sense and simplicity. They develop products that are simple, intuitive, and really easy to use for lots of people.

Products that have sense and simplicity are more easy adopted by your target audience and therefore more and more people are going to start to use them.

In figure 8, you can see there is an optimum balance between information and functionality of products. It clearly shows that if you give people too much information, features, or functionality to the point where people have to read manuals or follow training to use it, then people don't like it and they won't adopt your product at the rate you want them to. At the other end of the scale, if you give people too little information and not enough functionality to achieve their basic objectives, people don't like that either. Just like Goldilocks and her porridge, you have to get the bowl just right. You need to give them just the right balance of features to do a specific job and people will like it. Okay, there'll always be tech geeks and IT specialists who like to tweak any tiny detail, but getting the balance right will see that the majority of your target audience will be served.

We have used Apple's iPad as an example before. It demonstrates the point well; you can't do everything with it (the interface protects you from going deep into the operating system), but you can do a lot of things with it, and for 80% of the people that is more than enough.

A two-year-old kid can work it without any help from his parents, older people without any computing experience can do things on an iPad, many disabled people enhance their communication and learning capabilities with it, and even professionals can use them for pretty complex tasks. So when designing or developing a new product or service, make it 100% relevant, make it as simple as possible, and give it lots of sense!

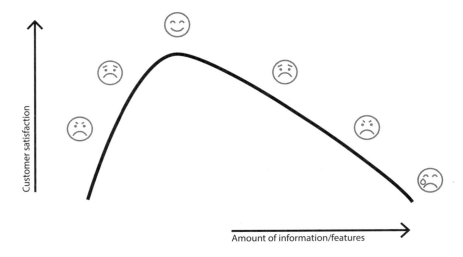

Figure 8: Sense and simplicity curve

The Path of Least Resistance

Nature is highly efficient (or lazy, if you prefer to think of it that way) and always takes the path of least resistance. It consumes less energy and fewer resources that way. Water will always flow to the lowest point it can reach, and even slime mould with no central nervous system will take the shortest route from A to B to find food and distribute the nutrients. We humans also prefer to choose the easiest route, the one that achieves the maximum output with minimum effort.

Increase Motivation and Reduce Friction and You are On to A Winner

Why walk for a day for water if you can live near a river and have all the water you need at your disposal? The design of great products and services works the same way; it's vital to keep in mind that people always prefer the maximum output for the minimum amount of effort.

When you design a new product or service for your target audience, it's of key importance to understand that every small action you ask of them that's not aligned with their own intrinsic needs, motivation, or natural behaviour will add a level of friction into the equation. They might not consciously notice it, but that little bit of friction will reduce the usability and uptake of your product.

People are naturally lazy in nature, so every action you give them should pay them back with some sort of benefit or reward that has some sort of relationship to the amount of effort they invested. Why should they do something for you anyway? People will only consistently do things because they benefit from it themselves. When you fully understand this principle, you can start to design your products or services more from a more human perspective.

During every process people have to go through a series of steps, and every step is a possible source of friction – whether it's downloading or installing an app, searching for information, visiting a website, submitting information in a form, searching for and buying a product, paying for a purchase, you name it.

So during any development work it's going to help you create a better product for people by doing everything you can to reduce the number of steps in any process down to an absolute minimum. After that, the next stage is to try to reduce any friction inside each individual step down to an absolute minimum.

The more powerful our technology becomes, the more flawless (automated) processes can be, but with the current state of technology there will always be small points of friction to overcome, and we have to work within our current constraints. As we get better and better we will be able to remove many of the constraints altogether.

Getting People Over the Finish Line

How many people back out of purchasing a product at the last minute? How many abandoned shopping carts are there every hour, day, week, or month?

Getting people to complete a transaction, finish playing a game, read a book until the end, or complete any manner or things is a perennial challenge. It can be difficult to keep people motivated to finish any process when the initial rush of interest has topped out. A couple of years ago, there was a big hype around the idea of gamification. In essence, it was all about using the psychological triggers that were also used in video and other games and incorporating them into all kind of business processes, products, and services. Basically, gamification was all about incorporating the human psychological triggers that are universal and independent of culture, age, or education and using those triggers to your advantage by manipulating customers to finish a specific process.

The hype is now over because many of the triggers were used in the wrong way and in the wrong place; but if you learn to use these triggers in the right way, you can really engage people.

In what is now an old study[43] ('MDA: A Formal Approach to Game Design and Game Research'), the authors, Robin Hunicke, Marc LeBlanc, and Robert Zubek, pointed out there are eight basic psychological triggers that motivate human beings intrinsically:

1. **Sensation:** Everyone is, in a sense, looking for a form of thrill. This gives us a kick and makes us feel that we are alive.
2. **Fantasies:** Everyone has certain fantasies that allow us to escape to a world of make believe.
3. **Stories:** People love stories with a beginning, climax, and an end, and it doesn't matter if the stories really happened or not.
4. **Challenge and competition:** People like to be challenged; people want to prove themselves naturally. But if the challenge is too big, we don't dare to enter; if the challenge is too small, we are not triggered to engage.
5. **Friendships:** Our social relationships are very important; they give us the feeling that we are part of something bigger than ourselves.
6. **Discover and explore:** We all have a certain degree of curiosity that entices us to explore new places and invent new ways to do things.
7. **Expression:** A sense of identity, self-expression, and recognition is important for us all. We have a desire to express ourselves to confirm who we are.
8. **Ranking:** Having a level of reputation and status gives us more confidence and respect within a social group.

Beside these eight universal triggers there are more basics to consider, including the fact that humans process visual information much faster and more efficiently than text-based content. That means that providing engaging visual interfaces that are very intuitive to use reduces friction and improves understanding. Our sensory preferences mean that colours, shapes, and sounds have a deep impact on how we behave and make decisions on an unconscious level. Possessing and applying this knowledge in the right way gives you a significant disruptive advantage compared to people who are not aware of it.

---

[43] http://www.aaai.org/Papers/Workshops/2004/WS-04-04/WS04-04-001.pdf

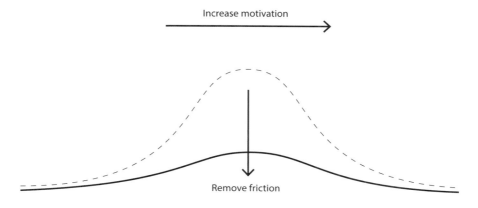

Figure 9: Increase motivation and remove friction curve

Successful disruptive organisations use one or more of these universal human triggers to engage their audience intrinsically. They create digital solutions that are even more compelling to human beings. If you need inspiration, then you will find some of the best examples in the entertainment industry. Take a look at theme parks, movie studios, video games, and online games and see how they grab your senses and fully immerse you in their world.

Think Big, Start Small

Do you think Nature writes project documents, functional and design documents before it starts to innovate? Of course not ... no way!

The biggest mistake many companies and organisations make is to think big and to start big. Someone has an idea and the first thing they start to do (if the idea even becomes a project in the first place) is start to write huge documents, stack up the research, and to think and design every tiny detail of the entire idea/project upfront.

As we discussed earlier, it's inevitable that when you show these project documents to ten different people, every single one of them will have a different perspective of the content, and a different personal vision of the end goal you are trying to achieve. All the feedback from the ten individuals is based on the personal mental picture that either he or she created. The result is a massive number of potential variables, a whole host of different opinions and there is little chance that the mental picture of one person is the same as the mental picture in the mind of the other people in the project team. The result? Massive confusion and miscommunication and a project that fails before it even get started!

Every day, massive amounts of energy, time, and money are wasted in this exact way. It's happening inside companies, governments, almost every other kind of organisation.

It's the innovation equivalent of trying to ride a bike for a mile with your eyes closed. Trying to calculate every variable before you leave, trying to calculate the best possible angle and speed to reach a specific point on the horizon, riding as if you were going to ride in a perfect straight line. What do you think the chances are that you will reach your destination like that? It's going to be almost impossible, because you can never predict all the variables (wind, tyre pressure, deviations, imperfections in the road, etc.). You will probably fall off the bike after a couple of metres, and I wouldn't be putting my money on you ever reaching the point on the horizon that you had set your sights on.

But there is an alternative. The one we would use naturally. That's to simply keep your eyes open, just start cycling and make small steering adjustments on a continuous basis. The chances that you will reach that point on the horizon will probably increase a million times – not by riding the perfect straight line but by continuously adjusting your direction and adjusting to your environment as you go.

This ability to developmentally adjust as the situation demands is exactly what Nature and disruptive organisations have in common. They both ride with their eyes wide open and make small adjustments as they travel.

They both think big, but start very small (on a subatomic or cellular level). They often start so small that you wouldn't even call it a project.

When you start to experiment, your most important goal should be to learn from the experience and gather valuable feedback that you can use to bring increasing levels of focus to the experiment!

That is exactly what Nature does best. When you master that, you could be the next innovative disruptor in your industry; and no one will have even seen you coming.

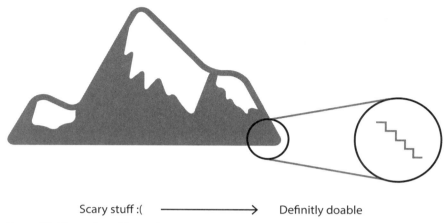

Scary stuff :(————————→ Definitly doable

Figure 10: Mountain vs. First stairs

Innovate like Nature Does

Nature does her experiments on a monumental scale. You could describe her efforts as massive parallel experimenting. Some of her experiments succeed and others fail.

The experiments that succeed get more energy and focus, and the experiments that fail are killed. Nature proves that this is a very efficient way to innovate, and she tries many new things at the same time and perseveres with the successful ones. Successful disruptive companies mimic Nature and experiment on a massive scale all the time.

Every idea is built on assumptions, and big ideas are based on a big stack of assumptions. So how do you prove if the initial assumptions are right? What disruptive companies do is that they start by creating a small prototype, and that prototype represents or proves the biggest assumptions or risks in their initial idea. Then they show the prototype to employees and customers at a really early stage and ask them for feedback. That way they get to prove their assumptions are right (or wrong!) at a really early stage. From there they can develop and improve their prototype based on actual facts from their target audience. After a while, it's possible to become so comfortable with the process itself that it becomes easier to increase the number of experiments, which is exactly what Nature does. Successful disruptive companies already work like this (for example, Google's holding company Alphabet has a massive number of start-up companies in play at any one time, with each of those running many experiments, product tests, and market tests). That's a far cry from what many companies do right now, which is build things based on their own assumptions.

If you're able to learn that quickly from your audience, you can gather massive amounts of factual feedback and that helps you to adapt to the needs of your environment (your target audience).

When you have the fundamental structures in place to manage this process well, then your company starts to behave more like an organism does. Organisms learn fast and adapt to their environment, and as you probably know, organisms that can adapt quickly to their environment have a much higher chance of survival than organisms that don't.

The Exponential Organisation

Is your organisation already organised in the same way as one single organism? Is it able to evolve at an exponential speed? Probably not! Very few companies are, especially more established ones.

Are You Going to Make Waves – Or Get Washed Away?

So what questions could you ask yourself to diagnose just how adaptable and scalable your organisation really is at this moment in time? Here are some good diagnostic questions to help you see where you are right now.

Wave 1.0 – How strong is Your Cultural Layer?

How solid is the foundation of your organisation? What kind of people are you hiring at the moment? Do you hire people with an entrepreneurial mindset who are open-minded to new solutions?

Are you hiring people (or do you have access to people) who are not scared of new technology, but instead embrace it? Do you encourage people to experiment and make mistakes, or are they discouraged from trial and error? And, how would your people answer that question if I asked them directly?

Do you focus on people with social and technical skills that appeal to a higher purpose that is aligned with your bigger organisational purpose? Do you have the right culture in place (which is a big challenge if you already have an established culture) to create the foundation for the next layer?

Wave 2.0 – How Strong Is Your Infrastructure Layer?

Have you recently used any tools, for example things like the business model canvas (that you can find on www.strategyzer.com/books/business-model-generation) to create an overall organisation infrastructure that suits your employees, customers, and partners best? Remember, the only constant is change.

Is your hard infrastructure flexible enough that it can constantly adapt to the ever-changing environment? Do you already use new operating systems to structure your organisation? Take a look at systems like Holacracy (www.holacracy.org), a new way of running an organisation that is inspired by Nature. Holacracy divides your organisation into small cells and gives your organisation a flexible infrastructure with clear roles and accountabilities. Individuals have the autonomy to solve issues locally and directly without bureaucracy. These kinds of business operating systems give your organisation the ability to evolve continuously; implementing Holacracy means you never have to reorganise again, because the system reorganises itself on a weekly basis. Many organisations in Silicon Valley (and elsewhere) have already implemented these kinds of organisational operating systems.

Wave 3.0 – How Strong is Your Information Layer?

Do you have an information system that provides you with real-time information about your organisation? Just like in an organism, it's vital that you have some kind of nervous system and senses that connect all the processes and hardware and sense what state the organisation is in at any moment in time. How good, actionable, accessible, and visible is your information? Does your organisation have smart dashboards with real-time information about processes?

Wave 4.0 – How Strong is Your Automation Layer?

Does your organisation have some kind of automation layer in place that automates all the information flowing through the organisation? And does this automation software automate the right kind of processes, so that the people in your organisation are able to focus on their work, their social and creative skills, learning brand new skills, and fulfilling their purpose?

Wave 5.0 – How Strong is Your Social Layer?

Does your organisation use internal social platforms to interconnect people inside the organisation so they can share ideas and knowledge in real time and act like one organism? Is your organisation using and leveraging the power of the crowd and communities on social media platforms? And does your organisation use social platforms to exchange information with people outside the organisation to get a better understanding of your environment?

Wave 6.0 – How Strong is Your Learning Layer?

Does your organisation have the right algorithms in place to learn and adapt to its environment at the speed of light?

Does your organisation use AI-powered business intelligence tools and smart algorithms to be able to adapt to your fast-changing environment? Does your organisation leverage smart AI platforms and ecosystems from the big players like Google, IBM, Microsoft, and Salesforce?

Wave 7.0 – How Strong is Your Creative (Imagination) Layer?

This is yours to create. The future rests with people like you.

As you have read this far, it's clear that you are one of the people who wants to make a real difference, and you have the power to do it.

Does your organisation have a solid vision of the future? So what are you going to co-create? What platforms are you going to create or be a part of? What part are **you** going to play in our future?

That's a question that each and every one of us has a duty to answer, and, for the first time in our history, we have the opportunity to play a part that's bigger than any previous generation could have ever imagined.

The Creative Revolution is Coming

So let's wrap up with an overview of the big picture.

I believe that as we move through this century we are going to see changes at a rate that we have never seen or experienced before.

We have been through many innovative waves in our recent history. We saw a Wave 1.0 shift with the Agricultural Revolution; that's where we mimicked the behaviour of cells and learned to cooperate to solve the challenge of getting food to all of our neighbours to help our collective survival.

We saw a Wave 2.0 shift with the Industrial Revolution; that's where we mimicked the behaviour of the vascular systems of plants and animals. This is where we were able to get further reach and start basic automation that gave us a massive explosion in growth and efficiency.

We saw a Wave 3.0 shift with the Information Revolution, where we mimicked our own nervous systems to create telecoms and computer networks that transformed our ability to communicate.

That led to the build-up of Wave 4.0, where we were able to take automation of processes to a new level that wasn't just physical. In the same way that evolution gave us automated processes with our reptilian brain, during Wave 4.0 we saw the true start of the information technology revolution that changed the way most of us lived and worked.

We have lived through the birth of a Wave 5.0 explosion, a world of social sharing. We have watched as the dramatic rise in social media has changed everything. It's very similar to the natural pattern as seen during the mammalian explosion millions of years ago. Wave 5.0 saw the power of the group helping to empower individuals. Our most recent Wave 5.0 has resulted in ever greater transparency in our world and an increase in collaboration. We are also witnessing the struggles of big government and organisations to change in the new landscape – but the future is clearly a collaborative one. Shared data, shared solutions, and shared ideas.

Wave 6.0 is where I believe we are right now. We are at a new juncture. We stand at the evolutionary equivalent of what nature created when she gave organisms a neocortex, the part of us responsible for our complex problem solving ability. Wave 6.0 fired up the start of our Intelligence Revolution. It's where we are seeing the fastest developments in machine learning, artificial intelligence and deep learning. These technologies that are going to transform the world we live in and they are going to do it at an exponential rate. Change isn't going to take generations this time around.

With the speed of our computers and the ability to collect, store and use digital data, we are going to see our technological universe expand and speed up at an exponential rate.

So where does that take us next? Well, that might be up to you! What happens in Wave 7.0 is currently residing in someone's mind; maybe yours. We are poised on the edge of an explosion of creativity. Wave 7.0 is going to herald an new era and a creative revolution.

Right now it's time to nurture the imaginations of our children and young people and we need to re-learn how to dream again ourselves. It's time for us to transcend the physical, just like our technology has. So as we near the end of this journey together, it's time to reflect on where we started and bring the story full circle.

Six years after the devastating news of my daughters terminal diagnosis, a combination of technology and a team of incredible people changed everything. We were able to reduce the stress on Lieke's body enough to give nature a chance to heal her. Progress was slow at first, but over time, cell recovery and healing went exponential. Now, the medical team call her a "non-scientific child" and they can't explain the turnaround. Lieke is 6 years old and no longer lives with a terminal diagnosis. She has regained the right to an intensive care bed if she ever needs it. She is an active, happy little girl who goes to school, does gym and takes ballet classes. Her life sentence has been removed, and a new life gifted to her in its place.

Every day her recovery continues to inspire me and she has become a beacon of hope for others. Together we all have the power to learn from nature, create things of beauty and live a life of purpose. We all have the power to change our world. My message is that we can do it together. So, where shall we start?

From Idea To Action – The Next Steps

It's one thing to know **why** we need to innovate and change, but it's much more difficult to know **what** to do, and even more challenging to know **how** to do it.

As the word spreads about the principles of Humanification, I am surprised that so many organisations are struggling to understand the scale and **Nature of the Problem** that they are facing. There seems to be a disruptor around every corner and there are many leaders who are unsure about how they are positioned to survive the next disruptive tsunami.

Staying innovative, relevant, profitable and meaningful is not an easy thing to do. It can be especially hard when you are on the inside an organisational bubble looking out; and the bigger the bubble, the harder it is.

It is clear that this book has opened a serious discussion and people are asking for practical help to ensure survival and move towards their own brand of digital disruption.

More practical tools are certainly needed so that the principles of the 7 waves can be applied in practical ways, and there's now team riding the wave with me.

Introducing The Humanification Institute

I'm pleased to announce the creation of The Humanification Institute. I believe this is a major step to helping leaders and teams to understand the true nature and scale of the challenges they face, and to help them uncover opportunities for exponential growth.

The purpose of the Institute is to develop and deliver naturally inspired solutions. My vision is that it will be the hub for solving real world problems and business challenges in a practical ways.

If you are ready to take the first step on the journey and ride the next wave, you are welcome to join us. We have created a free self-assessment for you so you can discover out how ready your organisation is for an exponential future. It's available online and with our complements.

www.humanification.com/nextstep

About the Humanification Institute

The Institute is the hub for our ideas, tools and people who are passionate about applying the principles of Humanification to organisations all over the world.

It's the place where great people with new ideas and groundbreaking technologies come together to truly help others understand **The Unique Nature of the Problem** and meet their big challenges head on.

Our goal is to help determine each unique roadmap to a million individual success stories, all inspired by nature.

The purpose of The Institute is to be a catalyst and to provide you with the tools you need to anticipate and ride the exponential wave. We bring together the brightest minds, the willingness to experiment and groundbreaking thinking strategies for you to become more innovative.

We have a whole host of exciting ideas we want to bring to you via the Institute;

- The Humanification Think Tank for CEO's and senior leaders
- The Research lab
- The Humanification Inspiration update about new disruptive technologies
- The Humanification conferences
- Live and online events that can reach audiences globally
- A suite of online tools
- Digital disruption workshops
- Purpose and network organisation scan
- Online resources

Together we can use the power of nature to provide the inspiration and solve the most complex of problems in the simplest way possible.

Take the Test!

The team at The Humanification Institute's research lab have put together a simple self-test to find out how ready for digital disruption your organisation is today, and how ready your organisation is to do the disrupting!

www.humanification.com/nextstep

Humanification: The Movie

Christian's dream is to create a world-class full feature movie/documentary about Humanification, so that the concept becomes even more accessible and engaging for a big audience. The vision is to create an engaging audio/visual tour using advanced and impactful emerging 3D graphics and video material. The journey will follow the seven-wave pattern from the first sub-atomic particle to molecules to cells, to humans and eventually to humanity. It will explain the relationship between technology and the society we live in today and will give us a glimpse into the future, where we will have a multi-planetary society. It will be movie about the impact of exponential technology on humanity and will show more people how and what we can learn from the parallels between biology and technology. The film is currently in the concept phase and Christian is looking for creative partners with an interest in co-funding and turning the movie dream into a reality.

Would you or your organisation like to participate in the creation of the movie/documentary?

Then visit: www.humanification.com

About the Author

Keynotes and Speaking

You can hire Christian Kromme as an inspirational speaker for your next event. Christian shows organisations how to turn technological change into a competitive advantage. He believes that visionary ideas have a lasting impact on people when they are delivered in a simple and engaging way. That's why he uses stories, engaging visuals and case studies to bring insights to life.

Christian Kromme is an experienced entrepreneur and futurist speaker in the area of exponential technology, disruptive innovation and strategy/vision development. During his presentations Christian takes his audience on a tour through our exponentially changing world in which more and more disruptive technologies and business models are driving a big shift towards empowered consumers and smart communities.

As a tech-entrepreneur Christian has participated in several successful 'disruptive' start-ups, often spin-outs in completely different industries. Each one has been focused on the interface between humans and increasingly useable technology.

Throughout the years Christian and Artificial Industry, the agency he founded, received several nominations and awards for its innovative vision and human-oriented approach, including the Shell LiveWIRE Young Business Award, the SAN Award, the Broos van Erp Prize and many others. In 2014 Christian sold the agency to a multinational and started to focus on his passions – speaking, writing a book, giving inspirational sessions and workshops on disruptive innovation and exponential technologies.

For more information, visit: www.christiankromme.com

A Message From Christian

I believe that if we can reach 1.000.000.000 people with the concept of Humanification, together we can make the world a much better place for us all. So when you have finished reading this book, please pay it forward by giving it to a leader, entrepreneur or policymaker in your personal network and help to spread the word.